From White to Black

The Story of a Black Family that Started off White

By

Tracy M. Lewis, Ph.D.

Edited by Geoffrey C. Fuller

Library of Congress
ISBN: 978-1499709902

3rd Edition: Printed 2021
Published through Create Space an Amazon Company 2014; published through Kindle Direct 2021.

Printed in the USA
Cover Design by Tracy M. Lewis
Cover Photo (Grace Grinage Pride and her daughter, Jane Pride)

DEDICATION

This book is dedicated to my great-aunt Bunch, my kindred spirit. Meeting you gave my life new meaning. I love you more than words could ever express.

To my grandfather, Edward Gartha Lewis: You are my favorite guy.

To Aunt Deekay: Thanks for your love and support. I smile every time I think of you.

To the rest of my Lewis (LOUIS) family: We are a strong, fun-loving clan with a proud and colorful heritage behind us and in front of us.

To Cornelia Grayson and Sylvester Grinage and Luke and Louisa: May we all be together again someday.

I was getting ready to go out the door to work when the phone rang. I didn't want to answer it, but something told me to pick up the phone. When I did, the voice on the other end said, 'Hello, Louise, this is Alex Haley.' I was shocked!

—Louisa "Bunch" King

Table of Contents

PREFACE

In 1924, Walter Plecker drafted and lobbied for *The* Racial Integrity Act, describing it as "the most perfect expression of the White ideal." Plecker directed offices under his authority to change vital statistic records and reclassify thousands of mulattoes (persons with mixed-race ancestry) *as Negro* without their consent and without notifying them. The existence of mulattos greatly disturbed Plecker, who was convinced that mulatto offspring were slowly contaminating the White race. Plecker referred to mulattos as *rats* that needed to be stopped. Many mixed-race families came under fire from Plecker, who delighted in informing such families that they were *not* White, *only* Negro. Shortly after, in 1930, the United States Census Bureau, *under pressure from White southern legislators*, stopped using the racial classification of mulatto altogether. As a result, the long social recognition of mixed-race people was lost.[1]

A staunch promoter of eugenics (a movement popular at the time but later discredited), Plecker intended to scientifically prove White racial superiority and thereby justify the marginalizing of non-White people.[2] Plecker's work on racial purity was praised by Adolf Hitler, who congratulated Plecker for being the first person to "get it right". Hitler acquired Plecker's publications and journal articles to disseminate to his up-and-coming political regime in the 1930s. Hitler began waging his own *ethnic* war ...on the Jews...similarly referring to the Jewish people as "a poisonous 'race,' which 'lived off' the other races and weakened them."[3]

Walter Plecker's belief that "one drop of Black blood makes one Black and only Black" was a lie perpetuated by Plecker and other white supremacists in America in their efforts *to purify* the White race. Sadly, their teaching still resonates across America today. Its residue still covers the minds of Americans, most of whom have never even heard of the *one-drop rule*. Yet, one-drop rule thinking is so ingrained into our culture that we don't even notice the ways we continue to perpetuate it...But if we pause and look closely... we can see it.

Introduction

You see, unfortunately, I am not Black. There are lots of different kinds of blood in our family. But here in the United States, the word Negro is used to mean anyone who has any Negro blood at all in his veins. In Africa, the word is more pure. It means all Negro, therefore I am not Black. I am brown.

—Langston Hughes

The subject of my book recently came up in a conversation I was having with two teachers around the copy machine at work.

"Hey, I heard you wrote a book. What's it about?"

Knowing their break was short, I tried to sum up the book with as few words as possible. "It's about me and my search to uncover my family history. I talk about how my family had been *White* for over one hundred years until the one-drop rule reclassified them as *Negro*."

"The one-drop rule . . . what's that?"

The teachers looked at each other for a possible clue as to what I meant, with no luck. They were clueless.

"Don't look at me," said one teacher.

"Well, I don't know either," said the other.

Then they looked back at me.

"Exactly," I said, smiling.

That response is typical. I don't mean that in a bad way. But it is rare to cross paths with someone—anyone—who has even heard of the one-drop rule let alone someone who can actually tell me what it means. Amazingly and sadly, the most insidious, malicious, and destructive practice in American history, next to slavery, is also the least talked about.

For over 300 years, the one-drop rule (also referred to as the one-drop law) was the acceptable practice in American society. Based on a person's physical appearance and genealogy,[4]America used the one-drop rule as the standard for determining who was White and who was Black. Whenever anyone was known to have or suspected of having even "one drop of Negro blood (meaning at least one quarter, one-eighth, or one-sixteenth)," that person was then classified, or in many cases *reclassified,* as "Negro."

I often use the *street-light rule* as a comparison to help people understand the cultural institution and practice of the one-drop rule in America. Over the years, I have heard people, both White and Black, sharing stories about the Street Light Rule. It is something we all had in common as children growing up in America. As kids we could play outside as long as we wanted . . . until the streetlights came on. Then all play would cease—games of kickball, basketball, jump rope, *everything* would come to a halt... And someone would yell, "Street light!" and kids would take off like *the Flash* in different directions, running for home.

Was the street-light rule written down anywhere?

Probably not.

Nonetheless, it was a law—an unspoken but generally

accepted practice that governed our lives, our neighborhoods, and our cultures.

In a similar way, the one-drop rule began as accepted norm, an unstated belief generally shared (mostly by Whites) and not written down at first. Later, this principle was codified, written down. White America used it to determine who was *White* and who was *Black* during slavery times. The rule went unchallenged for years until 1896 and the Supreme Court case of *Plessy v. Ferguson*. Homer Plessy, a multiracial Louisiana man with White features, challenged Louisiana's one-drop rule after he was discriminated against and refused a seat on a train. Plessy's case went all the way up to the United States Supreme Court, who "firmly and unambiguously endorsed the logic of segregation in the case of *Plessy v. Ferguson*"[5] by stating, "If one race be inferior to the other socially, the constitution of the United States cannot put them on the same plane."[6]

In the early part of the 20th century, the one-drop rule became *law* in many states. Tennessee adopted its one-drop statute in 1910, and Louisiana soon followed. Then Texas and Arkansas in 1911, Mississippi in 1917, North Carolina in 1923, Virginia in 1924, Alabama and Georgia in 1927, and Oklahoma in 1931. During this period, Florida, Indiana, Kentucky, Maryland, Missouri, Nebraska, North Dakota, and Utah all retained their old "blood fraction" *statutes* de jure, but amended these fractions (one-sixteenth, one-thirty-second) to be equivalent to one-drop.[7]

In the 1920s, two events occurred that added to the premeditated progression of one-drop rule thinking in America: the United States Census Bureau dropped the racial classification of mulatto (meaning a person of multiracial or mixed-race ancestry), and the Supreme Court of Virginia upheld the Racial Integrity Act in 1924, thereby outlawing interracial marriages. Soon after Virginia passed its law, other states began to pass their own *miscegenation* laws, strictly forbidding interracial marriages.

By 1930, thousands of White and Mulatto American families had been systematically reclassified as "Negro" or "colored." And with the aid of one-drop rule thinking, segregation and miscegenation laws across the nation were strictly enforced. Thoughtlessly and carelessly, families who had identified as White, as mulatto, and as Indian for generations, suddenly found themselves stripped of their ancestral identities, reclassified, and placed on the Negro side of the color line.

The fallout from the Supreme Court and U.S. Census Bureau's decision had a devastating impact on any person relegated to the Negro side of the color line. The weight of the Great Depression made it *even harder* for *non-whites* in a segregated America to find work. Jobs were scarce for whites let alone people of color.

While most states began repealing their one-drop laws in the 1960s, 1970s, and 1980s, the residue left behind continues to cover the minds of Americans and has had a demoralizing and devastating impact on thousands of American families... including my own.

For as long as I can remember, I had wondered about my family...I had wondered why we possessed such an extraordinary mixture of skin tones, hair textures, body shapes, and other features, not only in my immediate family, but also in my extended family. And the more family I met over the years, the more curious I became. I couldn't have known, early on, that the decades-long search for my roots would not only prove fruitful, but it would also illuminate some of the most vexing issues in society today.

By the time I moved to Virginia in 2001, I had been searching for almost twelve years, in every way possible, to uncover my family's history—with little to no success. It was as if my great-grandparents had never existed. For years, I had been interrogating and grilling the few family members I had contact with for information, to no avail. Then in my spare time, I would visit libraries and court houses to search through property records, newspaper articles, and whatever records I could find, always coming to a dead end.

Then I heard about a Mormon library in Charlottesville that had an extensive online family history collection, so I decided to stop by one evening. Two years later...I was still stopping by, searching through their family history database. And for the simple cost of $1 per visit, the librarians also gave me access to a *new* website called *ancestry.com*. The online databases made searching much easier. But they also made me more obsessed. After working all day, I would sometimes grab a quick bite to eat then head straight to the library, where I would spend hours searching through records. The librarians had come to know me well. Week after week, month after month, they eagerly assisted me in my quest to find some tidbit of information about my family. Yet, despite all my effort, each day I ran into a wall. I knew very little about my mother's family and even less it seemed about my dad's...it seemed a total mystery to me—a mystery I couldn't seem to solve.

Disheartened and frustrated, I laid my head down on the library table. Once again, I was the last person left in the library. It was dark outside. The library was about to close. And I had wasted another evening searching, with nothing to show for my effort. I was sad and I was weary. I heaved a heavy sigh then began to weep as I lay on the desk. A forever-present need to know deep down inside of me nagged at me with questions . . .

Questions I had been asking myself since childhood: Where did I come from? Who were my grandparents? Where did my great-grandparents come from? What were their names?

I so badly wanted answers.

Suddenly, a conversation between me and my Aunt Deekay from years earlier began to replay in my mind.

"Deekay, if Great-Grandpa Luke was Italian, then why is our last name spelled *Lewis*?" I had asked.

"It wasn't always spelled *Lewis*," she said. "The spelling was changed a long time ago. It was originally spelled *Louis*."

"That's it!" I shouted, jerking upright in my seat. My heart began to beat faster as I held my breath, quickly typing the name into the search field... *this time* spelling it... *Louis*. I hit enter and waited. . . Then suddenly, *whoosh,* the screen populated with names. And there he was, Great-Grandpa Luke.

Elated, I jumped up shouting *"Yes! Yes! I found him, I found him!"*

Overwhelmed by the excitement and adrenaline rushing through me, my emotions were uncontrollable. The librarians rushed over as I tried to wipe away tears rolling down my face.

Clapping their hands and patting me on the back, the librarians joined in my joy as I pointed at the screen, showing off my new discovery. They seemed to understand how badly I wanted . . . *nay* . . . *needed* to find something. I sat back in my chair speechless, looking around. It had taken fourteen years, but my breakthrough had finally come. Outside of the librarians, I was alone in my moment of revelation and excitement. I wished my sister, Tina, was there rejoicing with me. I couldn't wait to tell her. I couldn't wait to see the look on her face. I quickly started gathering up my papers and books. My heart was still beating with excitement. So many nights I had gone home empty handed. But that night was finally different. That night, I went home happy.

Chapter One: The Journal

> For mulattoes and Negroes, all rights were rooted in the past, in remote African ancestry. Ancestry alone determined status, which was fixed. A Negro could not buy out of her assigned race; she could not marry out of it, nor were her children released from its taint.
>
> —Christine B. Hickman

Several years ago, Aunt Deekay called me. I could tell by the tone of her voice she was upset.

"I finally sat the kids down today and told them they were Black...The boys cried."

"Deekay, why did you tell them that?" I asked calmly, trying not to sound shocked, even though I was.

"Well, I just figured it was time they knew."

"But Deekay, they're not Black. They're just as White as Donnie and *you*. And you're more White than you are Black."

"Yeah, I know, but that still makes me Black. Doesn't it make them Black, too?"

I could hear the confusion in my aunt's voice. Not agreeing with her had obviously thrown her for a loop.

"Deekay, you're thinking of the one-drop rule. And that was a long time ago. That law doesn't exist anymore. Your kids can be whatever they choose to be now."

"Really!" she said, genuinely surprised.

"Yes, *really*."

"Then why do people keep saying we're Black?"

I could hear the indignation and anger growing in her voice. And I was glad. I was also glad it wasn't directed at me. I took a deep breath, slowly exhaled, then answered her.

"Because they still believe it."

Aunt Deekay's words struck a nerve in me—*a raw one*. As I sat there listening to her try and explain her reasons for sitting my little cousins down and telling them they were Black, I got angry, but not at her.

Before 1930, individuals who were of mixed or multiracial ancestry, meaning White and Black or Black and Indian, were classified as mulatto. However, the states that adhered to one-drop laws would automatically classify mulattos as Negro or as colored, and any mulatto found trying to "pass as White" would face imprisonment, or a fine, or a public beating, or death. Beforehand, most states had limited trying to define ancestry before "the fourth degree," meaning as far back as great-great-grandparents.

I had been in conversations like this many times before, with so many different people, in so many different places. Now, here I was having one with family. In Aunt Deekay's mind one drop of Black blood made her Black *and only Black*, so therefore it meant that her children were also Black, *and only Black*. She, like millions of other Americans, was still under the influence of the one-drop rule.

My response had surprised my aunt. It had surprised me, too. But as much as she wanted me to agree with her, I couldn't. But I did feel for her and my cousins—my little blond-haired, blue-eyed cousins. Black barely added to the composition of Aunt Deekay's family. She had married Donnie, a French and Scotch, blond-haired and blue-eyed country boy born and raised in the hills of West Virginia. Yet despite this, Aunt Deekay, feeling the pressure from friends and family, believed the time had come for her to sit her multiracial (Black, White, Indian) and multiethnic (French, Scotch, Greek, Italian, Irish, Cheyenne, Black Seminole) children down and break the news to them.

"You're Black."

And they cried.

Long before I started my own decades-long search for explanations about my own unusual family, my great-cousin Grace knew Alex Haley, the author of the Pulitzer Prize winning book, *Roots.* Grace met Haley back in the 1970s through Harriette Calloway, the mother of Joseph Calloway, who was the filmographer on the TV miniseries of the same name. Harriette used to fill Haley's ear with stories about her cousin Grace—a Black woman who looked White. Harriette's stories about Grace piqued Haley's curiosity, so much so that he wanted to meet this Grace—a meeting Harriette was all too happy to orchestrate.

Leaving her home in Pittsburgh, Pennsylvania, Grace traveled to Harriette's home in North Carolina to meet with Haley. As Harriette had hoped, Grace shared the story of her family with Haley:

how her family had started off White and had been White for over one hundred years.

With features representative of her Scotch-Dutch ancestry, Grace could have easily lived her life as a White woman, in White society, but she didn't. She lived her life as a Black woman, the wife of a Black minister. Fascinated, Haley asked Grace to write down the story of her family, all the way back, as far as she could remember, so that he could tell the story of her family—*the story of a Black family that started off White*.

After returning home to Pennsylvania, Grace immediately set about the task of writing down her family history. She knew most of it by memory, from the stories her mother, her aunts, and her uncles used to tell about her grandparents: how her grandfather Sylvester had been a shoemaker in Pittsburgh and how her grandmother Cornelia had grown up in Virginia, the daughter of a Scottish plantation owner.

Grace began writing to relatives both near and far for information to add to the family history journal she had started. Grace's mother had fourteen brothers and sisters, all scattered about the states. She called her great-cousin, Bunch, in West Virginia to enlist her help. Bunch's grandmother and Grace's mother had been sisters. Grace told Bunch about meeting Haley and how he wanted to tell the story of their family. She asked Bunch to help her collect and write down their family history. Grace's excitement was contagious, so Bunch eagerly agreed to help. But Bunch's progress, compared to Grace's, was slow coming.

In an effort to motivate her cousin and speed up her progress, Grace enlisted the help of her new friend, Alex Haley, who had traveled to Pennsylvania to meet with Grace again, this time at her home. Grace told Haley about Bunch, how Grace had recruited her to help collect the family's history. She also told him that Bunch only lived a couple hours away from Warrenton, Virginia—the birthplace of her grandmother, Cornelia Grayson. Haley and Grace agreed that Bunch should go to Warrenton in search of Cornelia's long-lost relatives. They also agreed that a phone call to Bunch might help light a fire under her.

Haley made the call.

As she prepared to leave for work one morning, Bunch received a phone call.

"Hello, Louise. This is Alex Haley. I'm at Grace's house. We are talking about your family."

Bunch stood there, unable to speak. She had no doubt that the voice on the other end of the phone was Alex Haley, but she couldn't think of anything to say. Finally, she managed a very shaky greeting.

"Well, hello!"

Haley continued.

"Listen, Louise, I need your help. Grace tells me you live close to where your great-grandmother was born in Virginia. I need you to go there. I need you to track down some of your relatives who may still live in the area. Will you do that?"

"Why, yes, yes, I can do that," Bunch said, a little unnerved by his request.

"Good. Grace is working on her end. We need as much information as we can collect. You can help us. The story of your family is the story of a Black family that started off White. We need you to go to Warrenton, Virginia, to see what you can find out. Okay?"

"Okay, yes. I'll do it."

The conversation ended. Bunch hung up the phone, buzzing with excitement. Her heart was pounding. The phone call from Haley had done the trick. Her motivation level was

suddenly soaring. She quickly went to work writing down her mother and grandmother's family history. She also began collecting photographs, newspaper clippings, and other articles . . . whatever she could find. Her great-grandmother, Cornelia, had been born in Warrenton, a town about two hours away from where she lived, just over the mountain and across the state line. That's where Haley wanted her to go in search of answers. Out of curiosity, Bunch called a minister she knew of who lived in Warrenton. She asked him if he knew of any Graysons still living there.

"Oh, yes," he said. "There are a lot of Graysons in Warrenton—lots and lots of Graysons. Most of them are White or very fair-skinned, but some of them are Black."

The minister's response troubled Bunch. Her excitement was quickly dampened by the word "White." The thought of meeting *White* relatives in Warrenton made her cringe. And the thought of knocking on their doors made her cringe even more. Even though she also had light skin and White features like her parents, Bunch, like Grace, had lived most of her life as a Black woman, suffering much discrimination, hatred, and prejudice from both sides of the color line. The last thing she wanted to do was go knocking on the door of some long-lost White relatives, stirring up more hatred and resentment.

Even though Bunch knew how important it was to Grace and to Haley that she go to Warrenton, she couldn't bring herself to do it. She didn't want to risk a bitter confrontation. Therefore, she resolved that her role would be confined to writing and collecting information from her home on her side of the mountain.

Two years later, Grace became ill. Suffering from

congestive heart failure, she eventually took to her bed. She called Bunch and asked her to come visit in Pittsburgh. When Bunch heard that Grace was sick, she quickly made plans to go to her. Pittsburgh was only a few hours away across the Pennsylvania state line, so Bunch and her husband, Emmett, quickly made the trip. Bunch had grown very close to her cousin as they worked together, collecting, and recording the family history for Haley. But strangely enough, though they only lived a few hours away from one another, the two of them had never met in person—at least not as cousins. They talked quite often on the phone to one another. Then one day while talking, they discovered they had once lived on the same street at the same time, years earlier in Clarksburg, only a few houses down from one another. They had crossed paths many times, unaware they were cousins.

Walking into Grace's bedroom in Pennsylvania, Bunch exclaimed, "Well, I remember you. You used to live right there on Water Street, in the house next to the AME Chapel."

"Yes, I did. I remember you, too," Grace replied.

The two of them talked and laughed as they exchanged stories about family members. Then Grace gave Bunch the family history journal she had been laboring so hard to complete, making Bunch promise to keep it safe and to one day finish it.

Bunch promised.

Bunch left Pittsburgh knowing she would never see Grace again. And shortly after her visit, Grace passed away. Bunch never heard from Alex Haley again, but she kept Grace's journal safely tucked away in her closet—just in case. She often thought about what Haley had said about going to look for her long-lost relatives who lived not too far from her. And she often wondered who they were and what they looked like. But as curious as she was, she wasn't curious enough to get up the courage to travel over the mountain across the state line to find them.

Chapter Two: Heads California, Tails Atlanta

It is easier to build strong children than to repair broken men.

—Frederick Douglas

When I was twelve years old, my mother flipped a coin, "Heads Atlanta, tails California." California won and I ended up in Los Angeles, California—my destiny forever altered. Three days earlier, my cousin Diane and I had been waving goodbye to our family and friends from the window of a Greyhound bus as we prepared to leave our little country town in Clarksburg, West Virginia and travel almost 3000 miles away to a strange and foreign land.

Clarksburg had been my home for the first twelve years of my life. Now, I was standing on the sidewalk in front of my new home in south central Los Angeles, looking up at the bushy-topped palm trees lining the grassy island that ran down the middle of the block. It seemed surreal.

Life in South Central--what can I say? It could be fun. It could be scary. For me it was both. "It was the best of times, it was the worst of times," said Dickens, whose words perfectly captured my feelings. It was definitely the most confusing of times. My first night in Los Angeles was a nightmare. It was a summer night in July in L.A., so school was out. Most of the block kids had gathered at my cousins' house to meet and greet me—the new kid on the block. Terrified by the thought of meeting new people, I hid in the bathroom for over an hour, trying to get up the nerve to go and say hello.

Meeting new people was strange for me—I had lived in the same neighborhood, around the same people, for twelve years. Now I was starting all over again. I was trying to wait them out, but it wasn't working. They just wouldn't leave. It was awkward and nerve-racking. But finally, I screwed up my courage and emerged from the bathroom, forcing myself down the hall towards the sound of chattering voices. As I rounded the corner of the living room, I was greeted by ten or more smiling faces, all staring at me.

After introductions, I nervously tried to answer all of the questions they fired rapidly at me, but it was hard to keep up. Then, for a quick moment, the room grew quiet—an awkward quiet, which was then interrupted by a comment that became forever etched in my mind after an unidentified voice from the group shouted out.

"She talks White!"

Other voices began to chime in.

"Yeah. . . You talk like a White girl."

"You talk funny"

"Why do you talk so proper?"

And my all-time favorite, "Are you from the Islands?"

"What islands?" was all I managed to babble back at them, frazzled by the barrage of comments and questions.

I was from West Virginia. I didn't know anything about any islands. And nobody there had ever said I "sounded White." I didn't think I sounded White. And I didn't think I talked funny either. Proper, *yes*, but White, *no* . . . I got called *proper* a lot in West Virginia. People would often ask my mother, "Where did you get that proper-talking child?" Proper never bothered me.

Compared to the West Virginia drawl of my friends and family, yes, I did talk proper. I knew that... But I read a lot. In fact, I read all the time. I read anything I could get my hands on. Obviously, it showed.

I had been ambushed—caught totally by surprise. The questions from the kids on my new inner-city block made me uncomfortable and oddly self-conscious. So, I waited until the attention had shifted to somebody else—somebody other than me, then I snuck out of the room back to my hiding place in the bathroom. It was painfully obvious that I wasn't going to fit easily into their world. I was reasonably sure they didn't like me, which was unusual. In West Virginia, I had lots of friends. Everybody knew me. And everybody liked me. Now suddenly, in a matter of days, I was the unpopular misfit. Fitting in with the kids in my neighborhood became my new goal. Only I had to figure out how to do it.

My cousin Rodney was a drummer, who worked to my advantage. He had his drum set right in the middle of the living room. This made our house the preferred hang out for a lot of kids on our block. Rodney would often deejay, taking song requests as we all danced around the living room, making up dances as he played along on the drums. He was also an athlete and possessed the only basketball hoop on the block. In fact, he had built it himself. It sat on a platform with wheels. He could roll it out of the backyard into his driveway or onto the island in the middle of our block. As the guys played ball, I hung out with the girls, who gossiped and laughed as they talked about which boys were the cutest, as the music blared through the windows of our house into the street. And it became my job to make sure the music never stopped.

All the kids on my block were being raised by single moms. Rodney had become a big brother and father figure to most of the kids who came to our house. He was cool, funny, and caring. And he had a storeroom of knowledge when it came to life. On the other hand, everybody tip-toed around his wife—my cousin, Denise. She was the oldest of seven kids, so she was strict and formidable and knew how to bring order to a room really quick. Her very presence made everyone *mind their manners* whenever they came over, including the adults. But she would have given anyone the shirt off of her back if he or she needed it. As for me, the kids on my block liked me well enough to speak to me and invite me into their homes. This reassured me they didn't hate me.

In West Virginia, everyone spoke to their neighbor. Not so in Los Angeles. Whenever I waved and greeted people with a "good morning" as I walked down the street, I received suspicious glares and glances in return. However, my West Virginia charm quickly won them over. It wasn't long before I started getting waves and smiles back in return. Calvin, a teenage boy who lived down the block, appropriately nicknamed me, *Smiley,* which caught on quickly in the neighbor-*hood*. I didn't mind. Everyone had nicknames. Now I had one. It felt good to finally fit in.

My first summer in Los Angeles eventually came to an end. It was time to go back to school. Little did I know about the nightmare that was awaiting me. But I quickly learned. School in South Central was a battleground...A battleground for fashion wars that everyone waged. In South Central, your clothes, your hair, and your shoes said everything about you—cool, not cool, Poindexter, poor, welfare, drug dealer, gang member, etc.

From top to bottom, you had to look sharp. Everything

had to be perfectly color-coordinated—your socks, shoes, pants, shirts . . . everything. I watched my friends busily prepare their school wardrobes, giving amazing attention to detail and spending hours starching, ironing, and creasing their clothes, and polishing their Nike, Adidas, and K-Swiss tennis shoes whiter than white with liquid shoe polish. Designer jeans, colored corduroys, and Dickeys were the clothes *du jour* in South Central and at school.

My school prep consisted solely of organizing my school supplies. I couldn't relate to my block friends' ritual-like obsession with clothes and color coordination. I had never put a lot of thought into what I was going to wear before in West Virginia—so I figured, why start now? I had two pairs of pants, a skirt, two shirts and one pair of shoes to start the school year with, so I was happy. I knew we didn't have money to spend on a wardrobe full of clothes and shoes. My family worked hard, struggling to make ends meet. And we made do with the little we had—the West Virginia way.

Needless to say, my fashion choice didn't go over well at my new school on the first day. I stood out, *big time*. I knew right away that I was going to get a lot of practice in at being a loner.

In West Virginia, my days had consisted of playing outside with my best friends—Kim, Gina, and Josie, building cardboard forts in the backyard, climbing trees to pick apples, walnuts, and berries, swimming in the creek, and inner tubing down the river. Other days we would run around the town gathering up pop bottles to cash in for money to buy pop and candy, then we would lounge around at the library for hours, or hike through the woods up to Lowndes Hill to climb the lookout tower, or just walk the railroad tracks until we were exhausted.

In South Central that life was over, to my dismay. The constant threat of gangs and violence was all around us. And the repeated sound of gunfire late at night, seemingly every night, made me fearfully aware that "I was not in Kansas anymore." And school shootings and drive-bys were an all-too-common occurrence in South Central as gangs competed for recognition and territorial control. This made hanging out before and after school dangerous. Each morning I would hurry to school, half running and half fast-walking, constantly on the lookout for rival gangs prowling through the neighborhood in cars. Then, at the end of the school day, before the bell had finished ringing, I was out the front gate, leaving Bret Harte and 93rd Street quickly behind me as I ran for home.

A month or so after Diane and I stepped off the bus in Los Angeles, Mom arrived. Soon after, she and Diane moved to an apartment in Inglewood—the neighboring city to the West of South Central. Because of school, or so everybody said, I stayed with Rodney and Denise. My sister Tina had gone to live in DC with our dad. Tina and I had never been apart before. She was only a year older than me, so we were very close. Tina had always been there to look after me. Now she was miles away. I was heartbroken. I missed her terribly. And I missed my simple country life and my country friends. Every day I wanted to go home.

In West Virginia I had been outgoing and friendly. In California, I was becoming an introvert, slowly retreating into my own little world. Before long, the bossy, bold, and outgoing personality I had possessed in West Virginia was replaced with a timid, shy girl, who was afraid to venture off the block.

I rarely left the confines of my block without Rodney or Denise or my block friends by my side. And while I enjoyed the company of my block friends, hanging out with Rodney and Denise proved to be much safer. Ventures with my friends outside of our *hood*= meaning the few blocks of South Central that were designated as *Hoover Crip* gang territory, often resulted in confrontations with rival gang members or police officers, who repeatedly mistook us for a gang. This was probably due to the matching blue–and-gold-colored pants and shirts my friends *always insisted* on wearing wherever we went. Too many times, our outings resulted in fights, being shot at, and run–for-your-life foot chases that *thankfully* ended with nobody dead or in the hospital. Subsequently, I reasoned it would be wiser to explore the other parts of Los Angeles in the safer company of Rodney and Denise, or with my mom and Diane.

After my arrival in South Central, I remember commenting to my cousin Denise, "There sure are a lot of Indians in California." To which she replied, "They're not Indians, Tracy, they're Mexicans." I pondered the word Mexican. I had never met a Mexican before. In West Virginia, we had a lot of American Indians, but no Mexicans . . . at least not in my country town. Oddly enough, whenever I was with my mom, it never failed that a Latino or Hispanic person would try to strike up a conversation with my mom in Spanish. Mom's response was, amusingly, always the same.

"Why are you speaking Spanish to me? Do I *look* like I speak Spanish?"

"Uh...Yes, Mom, you do," was always my response.

Mom's indignation always struck me as funny. Her skin color and hair made her blend perfectly into the Latino and Hispanic culture of South Central. But Mom didn't see it that way.

After a couple years passed, I eventually began to venture out on my own more and more past the boundaries of South Central, taking the bus to the malls and restaurants in the surrounding suburbs of Los Angeles—Westwood, Century City, Redondo Beach, and Torrance—cities that became my New

Haven. Although the bus ride would take an hour or more to get to these places, I didn't care. With each trip, I discovered more life outside of South Central.

In a 2015 video entitled, "How to Tell Someone They Sound Racist," Nancy Giles of CBS Sunday Morning made fun of popular vlogger, Jay Smooth, for the way he spoke—seemingly because his light-bright-skin made her think he was a White man trying to *sound* like a Black man. She was shocked, however, when Jay Smooth responded by telling her, "It's also interesting because I'm actually Black, but you assumed otherwise." Jasmine Desmond-Harris, a writer for *VOX Xpress* online news magazine had this to say in response to the popular video: "It was a reminder of how complicated this whole race thing is, and how many different factors besides skin color inform identity. Lesson: you really can't look at people and decide what their background is or what they call themselves, ever—especially not on national television."[8]

I couldn't agree more. Life in South Central had made me aware of race and stereotypes and how tangled the two can get. And I have been trying to untangle the two ever since.

Chapter Three: The Segregation of South Central

A racist is one who despises someone because of his color, and a segregationist is one who conscientiously believes that it is in the best interest of Negro and White to have a separate education and social order.

—George C. Wallace, Alabama Judge, 1964

In 1998, I was staffing the crisis phone line in Nashville, Tennessee, at a prominent residential counseling home for girls and women, ages 13-28, when I received a call from a mom, clearly in distress. After a quick introduction, the mom told me she had a daughter who needed help. Then she began to fill me in on what was happening. As the mom shared, my heart went out to her and her daughter, who was suffering from drug addiction, depression, and cutting herself. The mom said a friend had told her about our girl's program and was sure we could help.

"I'm desperate!" she said. "I don't know what else to do."

I told the mom she had called the right place and told her how our program had helped many young girls.

"It sounds wonderful! It's just what I've been looking for."

I could hear *relief* in the mom's voice.

Then she added, "But I have one question. You don't have

any Black people there at the home, do you?"

Her question took me by surprise.

"Excuse me."

She casually repeated the question. "I said, 'You don't have any black people there, do you?'"

Hoping she wasn't serious, I responded.

"Well, yes, ma'am, we do."

"And the other girls there ...are any of them black?"

My curiosity had peaked. I returned her bluntness with bluntness.

"Yes, ma'am, a few of them are Black. Why? Is that a problem?"

Obviously, it was, but I asked it anyway.

After letting out a deep sigh, she said, "Yes, that is a problem. I don't want my daughter around anymore black people. They are the reason she is in this situation to begin with."

"Well, ma'am, I'm sorry you feel that way. But we do not discriminate here. We are open to girls from all races. And we have black staff members who work here as well, including *me*."

There was a long pause on the phone, and I held my breath, waiting to hear her response.

"Well. . . I guess I'll just have to keep looking."

Abruptly, she hung up the phone and never called back.

I deduced it was my "articulate speech" that caused her to assume I was White. I leaned back in my chair, laughing to myself, and feeling good for having made a racist look like an idiot. But my joy was short-lived. The reality hit me that there was a suffering teenage girl out there somewhere who was going to continue to suffer, simply because her mom didn't want her around black people. I felt sorry for the young girl. Her mom's prejudices and bigotry were standing in the way of her getting the help she needed. That weighed heavy on my mind.

Growing up in a little West Virginia country town, my life had been drastically different than that of my South-Central friends. In West Virginia, I had grown up in a small melting pot of people from different ethnic and racial backgrounds and, for the most part, we all got along. Interracial couples were common in our town, so I had my share of biracial friends. And I don't remember anybody ever making a big deal about it. Looking back, I assume it's because we were all struggling to make a living together, in the same boat—the *poor* boat.

Often, on a discovery tour to see what life was like beyond our tiny neighborhood, my friends and I would venture out to the surrounding towns. On our ventures, we would often stumble across, seemingly, all-White neighborhoods. One of my best childhood memories occurred on one such outing. My friends and I had been walking the back country roads for hours. We were on our way to visit their cousin who lived a few miles away, way out in the country. We had run out of food a while back and water too, so tired, thirsty, and hungry, we finally came to a pretty white house with a white picket fence around it. In the yard, pruning her flower bushes, stood a White lady. When the lady saw us, she smiled and waved, which prompted us to wave back.

"May we have some water," I asked nicely, hoping she would say yes.

The lady invited us inside and gave us all cookies, chocolate, and glasses of water. We looked quietly around at her beautiful home, careful not to touch anything. Then after a short time had passed, we said goodbye and resumed our journey as the lady waved us goodbye—four little Black girls, strangers passing through her all-White neighborhood.

That was my world for the first twelve years of my life. In that world, I learned to accept people the way they were—despite the color of their skin. In that world, I was comfortable around everyone and feared no one. My family members ranged from brown-skinned to light-skinned to light bright-skinned to White. I had a German step-grandma who came with German step-uncles and step-aunts. In that world, White people were not "blue-eyed devils" as I would later hear them referred to as by some of my block friends and by other South-Central inhabitants.

In South Central, things were different. In South Central, the one-drop rule was apparently present in the minds of my Afrocentric inner-city friends, who thought only in terms of Black or White. In South Central, the color line was clearly visible. And we lived on the black side of the color line. In South Central, there was only one world—a black one. South Central seemed like a land that time forgot, a world where segregation and racism (albeit reversed) were not only apparent but embraced: White people and anything representative of the White race and culture was *not* welcome.

My friends were proud to be Black and *only Black*. But for me, one-drop rule thinking was difficult. It meant picking which side of the color line I wanted to stand on. It meant segregation, which I had never really known. It meant thinking in terms of Black or White, which I had never had to do. And it meant turning my back on my West Virginian family and friends, which I wasn't about to do.

"Get back to your roots," I was constantly told by my block friends, school friends, and even by complete strangers who would quickly label me "White girl" as soon as they heard my proper dialect. On top of this, my choice of music was under constant fire from my block friends. Dawn, my closest friend on the block, was quick to educate me.

"People are gonna start calling you Oreo if you don't stop listening to that White music!"

"Oreo? What does that mean?"

"An Oreo is someone who is Black on the outside but White on the inside."

Dawn was the oldest girl on our block. She was funny and tough—a born leader. Everyone looked up to her and respected her, especially me. So, I listened closely to her warning, which both unnerved and angered me. I wasn't an Oreo. And I didn't want anybody calling me one. I wasn't White on the inside and Black on the outside. I was just me. I immediately hated that word!

In my friends' eyes soul, R&B, rap and hip-hop were the only acceptable sounds of the city. Anything else was foreign, sacrilegious, and would not be tolerated. And no self-respecting Black person would be caught listening to anything else. My friends made it verbally and demonstratively clear that there was no place in South Central for rock or pop music. An exception to this was rule, interestingly enough, was the rock group, Queen, whose songs somehow managed to slip through to become popular favorites in my neighborhood and all around South Central, even among the gang members, who especially enjoyed blasting the songs through the windows of their cars.

In West Virginia, I had grown up on a little bit of everything...pop, country, soul, *and* rock music. And my musical tastes didn't change when I moved to Los Angeles. I loved music, all music. My favorites being Michael Jackson, the Go Go's, Van Halen, Billy Joel, Madonna, Earth Wind & Fire, Motown, and *my all-time favorite*, Duran Duran.

My friends' criticisms of my music played like a broken record, as did their repeated threats to break my records. And I knew they meant it, so I kept my records safely out of sight whenever they came over to hang out. Once, however, I accidently left my Billy Joel album lying on the table in the living room. When Dawn spotted it, she snatched it up and ran outside. By the time I caught up with her, she had broken it in two and was stomping it into even smaller pieces in the front yard as everyone laughed and cheered her on.

"You need to get back to your roots! Black people don't listen to that kind of music." She once again admonished me. "If I see any more, I'll break them, too."

And she was my best friend.

I had no doubt she would make good on her threat, so I was extra careful to keep my records hidden and out of sight. God forbid she should break one of my Duran Duran records—that would have meant war.

Thankfully, Rodney and Denise never gave me a hard time about my music. At least I wasn't totally alone in my thinking. But my friends' words carried a lot of weight, so I kept my music to myself.

The reaction of my inner-city friends and others in and around my neighborhood to the presence of "anything representative of the White culture" was indicative of self-imposed segregation and what author, Guido Bolaffi, in his book, *Dictionary of Race, Ethnicity, and Culture*, refers to as *a mirror-image response* to racial segregation by Black people. The reaction and beliefs of my inner-city friends were reflective of the teaching and preaching of civil rights activists and Black community leaders, such as Marcus Garvey, Elijah Muhammad, and Louis Farrakhan... outspoken opponents of integration, whose teachings had resonated throughout Black communities since the 1940s, 1950s, and 1960s.

At the time of my arrival in South Central in the 1980s,

their message of separatism was still resounding in the inner city and could be heard and seen in the words and actions of my inner-city friends.

Get back to your roots!" my friend Dawn had yelled at me, with the expectation that I would rid myself of my White music and embrace the music of the Black race.

Marcus Garvey, a respected Black leader, and advocate of the *Back-to-Africa* movement in the early part of the 20th century, taught that segregation and territorial separation was not merely preferable but also a necessary prerequisite if Black people were to prepare to return to Africa. After Garvey's death in 1940, the then leader of the Black Muslims, Elijah Muhammad, echoed Garvey's anti-integration message in Black communities across America (leaving out Garvey's *critical* back-to-Africa context). Resurrecting the Black Muslim movement in America in the 1940s, Elijah Muhammad called *for the establishment of a separate nation for Black Americans.* He became known for his flamboyant rhetoric directed at White people, whom he labeled "*blue-eyed devils*."[9]

In 1965, Louis Farrakhan, a former member of the Black Muslims, rose up to become the leader of the Nation of Islam after the assassination of its former leader, Malcolm X, in February of that year. Farrakhan also held to the idea of separating Black people from White people.[10] And on June 24th, 2015, speaking to a crowd at the Metropolitan AME Church in Washington, DC, Louis Farrakhan stated, "I don't know what the hell the fight is about over the Confederate flag! We need to put the American flag down because we've caught as much hell under that as the Confederate flag!"[11] He added, "Who are we fighting today? It's the people that carry the American flag. What flag do the police have? What flag flies over the non-Justice Department? What flag flies over the White House?"[12]

His comments were met with cheers and applause.

By the 1980's, the message of anti-integration and separatism had been passed down for generations across the Black communities of America. As a result, my inner-city friends rarely ventured outside of the boundaries of South Central. On top of that, they had a strong dislike, and oftentimes hatred, for White people. And while my school and block friends, and even some adults, laughed and poked fun at the bow ties and dress suits worn by the Black Muslims, who made their presence known in South Central, my friends often, knowingly, and unknowingly, reinforced and disseminated their message of anti-white, anti-integration, separatism, and hatred for anything associated with the White culture.

The teachings of prominent and educated Black men such as Garvey and Farrakhan made them cultural icons. Up until South Central, I had never heard any of the teachings or views of Garvey, Muhammad, or Farrakhan. But in a family like mine that was threaded through with Black, Indian, White, Latin, and who knows what else, I often wondered what impact such racist and separatist views would have in a family like mine. Mercifully, their views were not the only ones available and stood in contrast to the views of other prominent and educated leaders and icons in the Black community.

Booker T. Washington was *the* most famous Black man in America from 1895 to 1915. He was also the most influential Black educator of the 20th century. Washington saw segregation as a detriment and a hindrance to the advancement of both Blacks and Whites—socially, morally, and academically. Also, in protest to segregation, Rosa Parks, in 1955, refused to give up her seat on a bus reserved for White people. She wanted to be able to sit wherever she wanted, *even if it meant sitting next to a White person*. Then in 1968, Martin Luther King, Jr. paid the ultimate price for taking a stand

and organizing marches and protests *against segregation* when he was assassinated on April 4th in Memphis, Tennessee.

Chapter Four: The White People Dilemma

> No one is born hating another person because of the color of his skin, or his background, or his religion. People must learn to hate, and if they can learn to hate, they can be taught to love, for love comes more naturally to the human heart than its' opposite.
>
> —Nelson Mandela

After one year at Bret Harte Junior High, I was enrolled in a new busing program, a program designed by the L.A. School District as a social and educational experiment for inner city minority students. Being enrolled in the program meant riding a school bus for an hour and a half each morning to *"the Valley"*—a conglomerate of cities in the middle-to upper-class to *upper-upper-class* suburbs in the San Fernando Valley, such as Encino, Thousand Oaks, Canoga Park, Tarzana, Van Nuys, Reseda, and Studio City.

The Valley had been popularized in movies, on TV, and in Moon Zappa's 1982 hit pop song, "Valley Girl," which I knew all the words to. I also read about *the Valley* in the Issues of *"Teen Beat, Tiger Beat,* and *Right On"* teen magazines that I saved up to buy each month. The Valley was home to a lot of singers and actors, including my favorite...*Michael Jackson*. Yet, although I often read about the Valley, I had never been there... So needless to say, I was excited at the thought of going to school there.

I welcomed any opportunity to travel beyond the isolated walls of South Central and leaving the overcrowded classrooms of my inner-city school was, for me, an added bonus. The same couldn't be said, however, for my block friends: Terri, Robert, Robbie, Mark, and Arty (all boys). Their moms had also volunteered them for the busing program, so they would be making the long bus ride with me. I was the only girl from our block enrolled in the program.

Our late-night porch conversations about our new adventure revealed the fear and apprehension of my fellow bus riders. For me, it was fear of the unknown—a new school with new kids and new teachers. But to the boys, it was fear of a new school... with *White* kids and *White* teachers... in a *White* neighborhood.

My friends didn't know anything except the inner city and our block. That was their territory, their stomping grown. Interaction and experience with other races and cultures, outside of their own (outside of the Latinos and Hispanics scattered amongst us) was rare. My friends only ventured outside of South Central when they had to, and almost always in a group. And from the stories they told of their ventures outside of South Central, the experiences had been less than positive. They talked often of being followed around by White security guards in malls or stores and not being allowed to even enter restaurants. Inevitably, my friends always concluded... "It's only 'cause we're black."

At the time, I had a hard time believing that was the case.

Disneyland Nightmare

The following summer, our block club took a trip to

Disneyland. The trip had been organized by Dawn's aunt, Delene Bobby— a civil leader, who lived on our block. She was also a paraplegic. A lot of my time was spent sitting with Delene, talking, taking notes, and helping her type contracts and letters to government officials. Delene would find jobs for us block kids and organize block events and skating parties to keep us busy and *out of trouble* during the summer. Our block club consisted of my block friends, me, and several other kids from the surrounding blocks.

For the Disneyland trip, everyone decided to dress alike—in blue or gold Dickeys and gold-and-white or blue-and-white sports t-shirts with our nicknames embossed on the back. To us it was harmless, creative, color coordinated fun...that would help us keep track of each other. However, in retrospect... *it was probably not a good idea*. To those outside of our neighborhood and outside of South Central, our blue and gold colors meant something else--they meant gang colors—*Crip colors,* more specifically, *Hoover Crip colors*, which was our cross street. Yet, while my friends would yell out and identify with Hoover Crips when they hung out on our block and at school... they were *wanna-bes.* They left the *real* gang-banging to the *real* gang-bangers, many of whom lived all around us in the neighborhood and on the surrounding blocks.

Apparently, our presence was quickly made known at Disneyland when, not even part way through our venture, we were descended upon suddenly by Disneyland security as we sat in the food court, eating, laughing, and talking *loudly*. I remember one of the older girls saying, "Look at all that security, they are chasing somebody!" We all turned to look like as a host of security guards descended upon us, quickly surrounding us.

"Get down on the ground!" they shouted, as the boys were pulled from our group, pushed to the ground, and searched, in front of an ever-growing crowd of onlookers. We were then hurriedly and aggressively marched passed crowds of people to Disneyland's front gate and promptly *thrown out*, with the directive to "leave and don't come back!"

Just outside the gate, on our left, were two more boys, also Black, kneeling on the ground in handcuffs as policemen stood over them. The boys were dressed like us, in Dickeys and two-tone t-shirts, but in different colors—*black and gray.*

As we all rode the bus back to South Central, I vented my frustration on the bus, but it only seemed to fall on deaf ears. I was sad, embarrassed, insulted, and offended by the way we had been treated... It was so unfair. We hadn't done anything wrong. Why didn't my block friends share my indignation and frustration? While initially, we had all been angry, my companions had quickly moved on to the discussion of where to order pizza from when we got home and to talking about the fun parts of the day. I, on the other hand, couldn't stop replaying the events of our Disneyland nightmare over and over in my head.

The Disneyland experience brought back a forgotten memory of a similar incident in West Virginia when I was eleven years old. My friends and I had been kicked out of the *Robinson Grand Movie Theatre* (the only movie theatre in town*)* after a Black person *reportedly* caused a disruption. The movie stopped, the lights came on, and the ushers went through the movie theatre pointing out every single Black person they could find and ordering them out of the movie theatre. *Now,* thanks to Disneyland, I had another memory *that would last me a lifetime.*

My friends' hadn't exaggerated. From then on, I believed their stories about being discriminated against when outside of our neighborhood, and how their interactions with the White race, more often than not, resulted in experiences similar to the one at Disneyland. Their experiences had left them, not only with a very bad impression of White people, but with a seemingly indifferent attitude after such treatment...as if they expected as much.

Even though poverty stricken, graffitied ghettos existed all over South Central, some just a few blocks down the street from our house in either direction, we didn't live in one. Nor did we live in the projects. Our inner-city block was nice, clean, well-groomed... and, during the day, somewhat peaceful. The gang violence and crime that plagued some of the surrounding neighborhoods rarely overflowed onto our block, due in large part to *Momma Queenie,* a nosey old lady who lived across the street from me. Momma Queenie was a tall, heavy set woman, who made it her business to patrol the street in her house-robe, day, and night, from her porch and by foot. Walking up and down the street, she was a one-woman neighborhood watch, always yelling at us "loudmouth kids" to be quiet and threatening to call the cops on anyone who ignored her.

Coming off the freeway for the first time into the Valley and turning onto the street leading to our soon-to-be school, Mulholland Jr. High, our hands, and faces were pressed against the windows of the bus as we all "ooh'd and ahh'd" the change of scenery before us. In contrast to some of the older buildings in our own neighborhoods with gang names and symbols painted on them, and the clunkers, low riders, and other American-made cars we saw everywhere in South Central, on the Valley streets we saw luxury—Benzes, BMWs, Volvos, Jaguars, and limousines.

Each time a car came to a stop next to the bus, I found myself glancing into the car's window, looking for and hoping to see a Black face. As we pulled into the parking lot of the school, the White students stared at us from the open walkways and through the fence as we stepped off the bus. But their curiosity made even me uncomfortable. I wanted to yell, "Go away!"

Once again, I felt like an oddity, but at least this time I wasn't alone.

My Valley school experience quickly began to reshape my world view just as much as the South-Central neighborhood I went home to every day. Going back and forth from the inner city to the Valley each day made me constantly aware of how much better life could be. Soon, I began to dream...I began to dream myself past the boundaries of South Central.

Despite my shy and timid personality, I could make friends easily enough in familiar and comfortable surroundings. I breathed a huge sigh of relief when I saw that the White students' wardrobe consisted mainly of jeans, t-shirts, vans, and flip flops. Here, at my new Valley school, my cheap clothes and shoes would be just fine...I was already feeling *right at home*.

Not long after my arrival at Mulholland, boys began asking for my phone number...*White boys.* This was a new experience for me. But while I was flattered by their attention, I was cautious.

"No, sorry," I would say. "I can't have phone calls from boys."

My answer was always the same. I didn't know if it was true or not. *I had never actually had a call from a boy, White or Black.* However, the thought of having a boy...any boy... *especially* a White one, calling my house was unnerving. If my block friends found out, I would *never* hear the end of it. The warnings and constant negative comments about White people, *especially White men,* let me know from day one in South Central that Black women and White men were not supposed to mix. And *the glares, stares,* and *shouts* that I saw and heard from my South-Central bus mates whenever a White boy said hello to me, smiled at me, or God forbid stopped to talk to me, made me aware that I was being watched...so I was paranoid and forever conscious of the fact that my black brothers and sisters would not approve.

"Don't ever marry a White man!" was a very common phrase in my South-Central neighborhood, often spoken by the boys and men on and around the block. The phrase usually followed, or was inserted into, any conversation concerning the many injustices, *past and present*, that had been perpetrated by White people on Black people. It also followed the negative portrayal or treatment of somebody Black on television, on the news, or in the newspaper. Inevitably, at some point in the discussion, amidst the anger and outrage, someone would decree in the midst of all people present, both men and women alike, "Don't ever marry a White man."

If anyone disagreed, I never knew it because nobody ever spoke up. I most certainly disagreed. But I kept my mouth shut because the comment was always directed at us girls, *mainly me*. I was the *only* one on my block whose walls were adorned with pictures of pop stars, rock stars and actors, most of them White boys. This was well known by my block friends—therefore, they persistently felt the need to *save me* from the evil influence of White people, especially White men.

The perspective, however, of my block friends and neighbors irritated me. Early in life, I had learned the definition of hypocrisy ... A *hypocrite* [hip-uh-krit] is a person who feigns some desirable or publicly approved attitude, especially one whose private life, opinions, or statements belie his or her public statements. The perspective of my block friends and neighbors was a clear-cut case of hypocrisy, seeing as the guys never applied this philosophy to themselves. They never turned to each other and said, "Don't ever marry a White woman."

It was a double standard if ever there was one.

But at fourteen, I wasn't thinking about marriage. I barely thought about boys. Because whenever a boy did approach me, Rodney would grill him with questions and a speech about his intentions. Needless to say, on my block, I was relegated to being the perpetual little sister that they dared not approach.

At my Valley school, I acquired a newfound boldness. Soon, I began to care less about what my inner-city friends thought. And I resolved that I would like whoever I wanted to like and whatever I wanted to like—*and that was that*...Even if it meant being a *loner.*

Besides, I always had Rodney and Denise. They were my best friends. Around them, I was free to just be *me.*

Chapter Five: The Age-Old Skin Color Issue

Through all this ordeal his root horror had been isolation, and there are no words to express the abyss between isolation and having one ally.

—G. K. Chesterton

I remember when Spike Lee's movie "School Daze" was released in 1998. It stirred up a hornets' nest of controversy in that it was one of the first movies to shine the light on the tensions that existed (and still exist) between light-skinned Blacks and dark-skinned Blacks. (I use the term Black, not African-American because I am referring to a problem that exist within the Black race as a whole—and not just in America.) While I wasn't a big fan of the movie, I did applaud Spike for calling attention to an age-old bigotry residing within the Black culture. I thought it was time somebody talked about it.

The skin color issue in America can be traced back to slavery times when slave masters would separate the darker-skinned slaves (whom the masters derogatorily referred to as *field niggas*) from the light-skinned mulatto slaves (whom the masters referred to as *house niggas*). This practice planted seeds of jealousy, envy, prejudice, and hatred among the slaves and created a feeling of superiority among the light-skinned slaves who believed they were highly favored by the masters. Inevitably, the practice also created feelings of inferiority and resentment among the darker-skinned slaves who believed they were less favored by the masters.

Spike Lee recreated this separation practice during the making of *School Daze* by separating the dark-skinned Black actors and actresses from the light-skinned ones, even lodging them in separate hotels. His purpose for doing so was to increase the tension and prejudice that still existed between the two groups, and he succeeded.

While there have been a few, the one-drop rule was not an issue that movies focused a lot of attention on in the 20th Century...not as much as other race issues. When I was sixteen years old, I remember my mother excitedly pulling off my headphones and dragging me into the living room one afternoon.

"Tracy, you need to watch this movie. It is so good," she said as she sat me down in front of the TV, all but ordering me to watch the Saturday afternoon matinee that was about to begin.

Seeing as she didn't give me a choice, I sat down, intrigued. My mother had never (and has not since) told me to watch anything. The movie was called, "Imitation of Life" and starred Juanita Moore and Lana Turner. In the 1959 movie, Lana Turner plays a struggling young White actress with a six-year-old daughter. She hires a live-in housekeeper—a homeless, widowed Black woman with a pale-skinned eight-year-old daughter. The daughter rejects her dark-skinned mother, runs away from home, and tries to live her life as a White woman. The movie reduced me to tears, and after it ended, I understood my mother just a little bit more. And why the movie meant so much to her. Her light skin had enabled her for several years to attend a segregated White school in her West Virginia neighborhood until she was eleven years old. Forced segregation soon put an end to that...And she, like many other mulatto children, was forced to attend the only school in town for Negro (or colored) children.

Growing up, I was the only female in my family with brown skin, so I became very aware of skin color at an early age. In a house full of light-skinned women with cream-colored skin, I forever felt out of place...forever the brown-skinned oddball. My Grandpa Smitty was my only dark ally. Born and raised in Atlanta, Georgia, his skin was so dark it appeared black. Whenever I got in trouble with Grandma Stella, which thankfully wasn't often, I would run and hide behind Grandpa Smitty, who always took my side. He would often whisper in my ear, "Our color is the best color." His words somehow made me feel better and always made me smile.

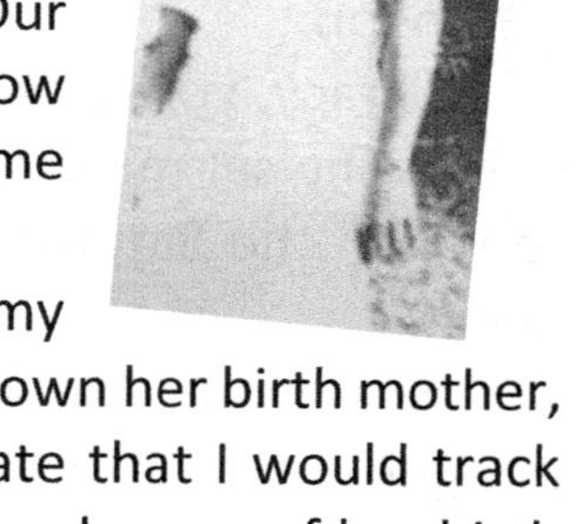

In reality, my Grandma Stella was my mom's grandmother. Mom had never known her birth mother, or her biological father. A birth certificate that I would track down almost forty years later listed the real name of her birth mom.

Grandma Stella was mulatto, mostly Cherokee and Irish with some African mixed in. And while she had long silver, gray hair when I knew her, people said younger pictures of her had showed off her bright red hair. I remember mom telling me how Grandma Stella hated her red hair and kept it dark, dark brown by washing it in ground-up coffee beans.

My mother was also named Stella. And like Grandma Stella, mom too had light skin and dark hair. Younger pictures of mom as a child showed her with two long black braids that reached all the way down to her elbows.

Growing up, as far as Tina and I knew, we had no other family in Clarksburg besides our Grandma Stella and Grandpa Smitty, and our mother, Stella—no cousins, no uncles, no aunts. Nobody. Our grandparents had taken over the task of raising us after our parents' breakup. With Tina and I nestled safely in the nest of her parents, our mother had hit the road, often traveling wherever life would take her. She would return home to settle down and work a job for a short time. Then, when wanderlust overcame her—she would hit the road again, off to another place. Likewise, our dad, Eddie, had also taken off and hit the road, traveling the roads as a bass player in a band.

Our dad was never talked about in our house. For Tina and me, Grandpa Smitty was "Dad." We had no idea what our father looked like because there were no pictures of him visible anywhere in our home. In fact, there weren't many pictures at all in our home. A house fire had burned our house to the ground when I was four years old, causing us to move from Northview, a tiny, all-White neighborhood just outside of town, to the Black side of town. Grandma Stella and Grandpa Smitty had lost everything in the fire. All they could afford on their social security and a retired coal miner's pay was a little shotgun house next to the creek (so-called because the house was so small, you could shoot a gun through the front door of the house and the bullet would go straight through out the back door). My mother had grown up in Northview. Living in town was quite different. Still, despite the smallness of our little house, Grandma and Grandpa worked hard to make it a home by building a fence and planting a garden in the backyard, next to a small apple tree.

Grandma Stella quickly established her presence in our new neighborhood. She was well respected, but she was also a force to be reckoned with and her temper became well known around town. She had a butcher knife collection, which hung on the kitchen wall. People knew she meant what she said. And they knew not to cross her. Sometimes women would run to our house seeking refuge from their abusive husband or abusive boyfriend. Grandma Stella would grab a butcher knife off the wall and storm out the door to go *have a talk* with the man. I never knew where she was going, but I never doubted she would come back.

At nine years old, my seemingly ideal childhood was suddenly shattered when cancer got the best of Grandma Stella. I watched quietly one afternoon as my unstoppable force of a grandmother sat quietly on her bed, laboring hard to breathe. I couldn't understand why she looked so worn out and tired. She never looked tired. Still, she tried to manage a smile when she saw me staring at her from the doorway. I went over to the bed and hugged her.

"Are you okay, Grandma?"

"I'm okay, honey. Go on outside and play."

Her weak smile dispelled my concern. I smiled back then darted out the front door to join my friends in a game of kickball. That was the last time I saw Grandma Stella. She was taken away to a hospital that day. Tina and I were never told where. But we waited every day for her to come home. We waited for her to come home and wash and press our hair, like she did every Sunday night as we watched "Wonderful World of Disney" on T.V. However, days passed, but still no Grandma Stella. And none of the grownups were talking. They weren't telling us anything. Then the news finally came as Tina, and I walked home from school one day to the sympathetic shouts of the neighborhood kids all along the way.

"Sorry about your grandma dying!"

Tina and I didn't stop to ask any questions. We were both secretly hoping it wasn't true. But when we reached home, Mom was waiting for us, with the official news... Grandma Stella wasn't coming home.

She had died in the hospital.

Tragedy birthed a revelation at Grandma Stella's funeral, when a pretty woman with dark chocolate skin like Grandpa Smitty's, sat down next to us. She had two older girls with her. But they didn't look like her—not even a little. One had White skin and one had light skin like mom and Tina. But I didn't recognize her. I didn't recognize any of them, neither did Tina. But the darker-skinned woman held on tight to my mother who lay across her lap, crying uncontrollably. The woman tried hard to comfort Mom. The two girls had wedged themselves down between Tina and I, hugging us close as Tina and I exchanged the same curious look.

"Who are these people?"

Not long after Grandma Stella's funeral, Mom moved us out of Grandpa Smitty's house, to the outskirts of town, into a small trailer park. Far out in the country in a community called, *Quiet Dell* (an infamous place widely referred to as *Murder Farm*). It was far away from our creek-side home with the apple tree in the backyard, far from my neighborhood friends, and too far from Grandpa Smitty, which saddened me.

Mom soon enrolled us in Stonewood Elementary, which I will forever refer to as "hell on earth." At Stonewood, my life changed... At Stonewood I received my first introduction to racism, discrimination, and segregation... At Stonewood, I counted one Black student in the entire school... *Me*. At least that was all I saw. And I looked really hard, every day, to no avail. Although Tina was Black, I didn't count her. At Stonewood, her light skin worked to her advantage...She blended right in—too well.

At my old school, Towers Elementary, each class was sprinkled with two or three Black students, mixed-race students, and American-Indian students all the way up to the sixth grade—enough to call it integrated. At Towers, my classmates and I had been friends ever since kindergarten or first grade. We all knew each other well...So skin color had never really been an issue.

At Stonewood, this was not the case. At Stonewood, I stood out. I hated it. And I hated the singularity of White faces, with no color mixed in. *Stonewood was strange... racially and culturally.*

Another first was riding the school bus each morning. However, our riding the bus proved to be providence for Tina and me. As we boarded the school bus that first morning, a teenage girl boarded the bus with us. She was thin and pretty, with straight black hair that hung in two braids all the way down her back to her hips. At first, we thought she was Italian...then American-Indian. We were sure she was one of the two. There were lots of Italians in Clarksburg. Lots of Indians too. By the girl's side was a small boy with wild brown hair, pale White skin, and bunches of freckles. Strangely enough, the two of them looked familiar to me. I had a feeling I had seen them before. But I couldn't remember where.

Tina quickly recognized the girl as one of the girls who had sat next to us at Grandma Stella's funeral. The girl recognized us, too. She smiled and sat down in the seat next to us. And the little boy plopped down right beside her.

"Hi, I'm your Aunt Starla—your dad's sister."

"Our aunt!" Tina and I said in unison then looked at each other.

We both had the same confused look on our faces. This news was a surprise to us both.

We all began to talk. We found out the little boy with Starla was her five-year-old step-brother, Mark, and that Starla was just a few years ahead of us at Stonewall Junior High. On top of that, her last name was also Lewis. After meeting Starla, Tina and I were all smiles. It felt good to know we weren't alone in the world anymore.

Starla found me in the hallway outside of my fourth-grade classroom later that same day. With her was another girl who she quickly introduced.

"Tracy, this is Mary Lewis, our cousin."

"You're a Lewis, too?" I asked, as I smiled up at her.

Mary was tall and thin. And, like Starla, she had light skin and long black bushy hair. I liked her smile and the fact that she seemed genuinely pleased to meet *me*.

After exchanging a few words, they returned to the junior high side of Stonewood. Smiling and happy, I counted... In less than a week I had gained an aunt and a cousin—both with the last name Lewis. But I wondered, where had they been all this time?

Having so few family members probably wouldn't have mattered so much if I hadn't been so isolated at Stonewood. I had been trying to keep a low profile and subtly make my way around the unwelcoming school. But there was Bobby Runyon to contend with. With his red hair, freckles, and raspy loud voice, he made up his mind he didn't like me the first time he saw me. So, he appointed himself my relentless tormentor on my first day of school.

"Hey, Black Rose!" Bobby hissed at me.

His little turned-up nose and sneer made it obvious he did not mean it as a compliment. Then on the playground during recess he started in again.

"Hey, Black Rose! Your sister's pretty, but *you'rrrre ugly*."

Each day he greeted me the same. And each day on the playground, skipping around, he taunted me with his little chant: "Black rose, Black Rose, Black Rose..."

I hated Bobby Runyon with a passion. I wanted to pound him into the ground. And I knew I could. At nine years old, I was a pretty tough kid, mainly because I had been fighting boys since age five. And I had an almost perfect win record. In my old neighborhood, kids would often pick fights with me in clans, so if you fought one, you had to fight them all. Tina and I didn't have any family to call for backup, and they knew it. So, they picked on us a little more. Life being as it was, I had to learn to fight really well, real fast.

I wanted to teach Bobby a lesson so bad...But I didn't. Why? *Because Grandma Stella didn't raise no dummy*. Even at nine years old I was smart enough to know that I was outnumbered...a foreigner in a strange land, with no allies. I only just met Starla and Mary. I didn't know them well enough to call on them for backup.

Life at Stonewood began to wear me down. Each day I found a place to cry alone, out of sight. I wanted so badly to go back to Grandpa Smitty's house, back to my old school, and back to my old friends. I hated my mother for moving us so far away. And I hated my sister for being able to blend in with her light skin. Life seemed good for her. But for me, not so much. I was on my own, enduring and suffering in silence.

Each day I sat on the playground alone. Each day I ate in the lunchroom alone. Nobody was brave enough to sit with the Black kid, or the *Black Rose* as Bobby Runyon had dubbed me.

Even Tina steered clear of me. Once I tried to eat lunch with her.

"Get away from me," she whispered.

Quietly, I withdrew, leaving her to eat with her new White friends, as I choked back tears, wishing for lunchtime to end as I sat alone, mad at my sister. We had always stuck together. Now, when I needed her most, she was pushing me away.

I began plotting my revenge.

"I'll get her. Just wait 'til we get home."

I knew how to get her back. All I had to do was call her *yellow*. Calling her yellow always made her angry. And sometimes it made her cry. She hated that word—*all light-skinned Black people hated that word.* Once, in my old neighborhood, I yelled *yellow* at a light-skinned girl after she made me mad, and I learned real fast how to quickly get into a fight. Then once, *and only once*, I heard Grandpa Smitty call Grandma Stella *yellow*. In a flash, she was after him with a butcher knife in hand. Grandpa Smitty took off running out the front door and across the front yard, with Grandma Stella right on his heels.

Thankfully, she never caught him.

Chapter Six: Door to the Past

When a man starts out to build the world, he starts first with himself.

—Langston Hughes

When my sister was nine years old, a White lady looked at her and said to my mother, "You can tell she's your daughter. She looks just like you."

Then the lady looked at me and politely asked, "And who do you look like?"

Her words stunned me. I sucked in my breath and shrunk away from her as I looked to my mother for an answer.

Indignantly, my mother informed the woman that I was *also* her daughter.

The woman's question embarrassed me and left me speechless. The truth was... I didn't know *who* I looked like. I was eight years old at the time. And while I had never met my dad, I did know his name— Eddie Lewis.

After we moved to the trailer park in Quiet Dell, more relatives suddenly began to appear in our lives, opening my eyes wider to the unique nature of our family. Denise and Rodney, cousins from my dad's side of the family, were just two of them. They soon joined Tina and Mom and me in our little trailer. Recently married at nineteen, Rodney and Denise became a permanent and welcome addition to our family.

Denise and her family had grown up with Starla and my dad. And she had eight brothers and sisters, which meant more cousins, which meant more allies.

One night, my new cousins piled me into a car with them and drove to a house in Eastview, another part of Clarksburg I had never been to before. We climbed what seemed like a thousand stairs and were greeted at the top by Starla. I usually only saw her on the school bus. Her sister Deekay also greeted us at the door. I instantly recognized her. She was the other girl who sat with us at Grandma Stella's funeral. Scooping me up into her arms, she gave me a big bear hug. She had held on to me pretty close at the funeral, too. I liked her right away.

As I sat on the floor of the small living room, I looked around, taking inventory of everyone in the room. My cousins I knew, and my two aunts I knew, but I didn't know the dark-skinned woman who kept staring at me and smiling. She was dark and pretty with a big, beautiful smile. But she kept looking at me, and it made me uncomfortable. I was a bit of a shy kid in unfamiliar territory. So, I tried hard to avoid her gaze. While everyone laughed and joked with each other, I stole glances back at her. She looked familiar, but I couldn't place her face. Then I remembered: She was the woman who had held my mother on her lap at the funeral.

Thirsty, I asked for some water. My cousin pointed me toward the pretty smiling woman.

She said, "Ask Aunt Deanny."

Nervously, I walked over toward the woman.

I asked, "Aunt Deanny, may I have some water please?"

"Aunt Deanny! Don't you know who I am?"

The room erupted in laughter, but I didn't know why. I looked at Aunt Deanny who still smiling at me.

Shaking my head, I said, "No."

I looked around the room at my cousins, who all sat

giggling and staring at us like they knew something I didn't.

"Do you know who Eddie Lewis is?" Aunt Deanny asked again.

"Yes. That's my dad's name."

"Well, that's my son. I'm your grandmother."

Once again, the captive audience broke into laughter. Apparently, that was the big something. That was the big secret.

Meanwhile, I stood there, surprised, and annoyed. I seemed to be the only person in the room who wasn't in on the secret.

I got my water and sat through the rest of the evening, both confused and happy. I kept stealing glances at my new grandmother as I sat on the floor at her feet. I believed she was my grandmother. I could tell. She was a few shades darker than me, but we looked exactly alike—our eyes, our smile, our cheeks, everything. And her dark skin reminded me of Grandpa Smitty, who I was missing terribly.

Excited to have my new grandmother, I was even more excited to finally have an answer to my skin color question. I was no longer the oddball in my family. Around Grandma Deanny, I fit in perfectly. And from that moment on, Aunt Starla, Aunt Deekay, and all my new cousins began calling me "little Deanny."

In less than a few weeks, the count had risen to two aunts, eleven cousins, and a grandmother to stand in place of the one I had lost, although no one could ever replace Grandma Stella.

Again, I wondered why I had never met Grandma Deanny before that moment. Where had she been for the past nine years of my life? Later in life, I would learn the answer to that question.

Apparently, my parents were high school sweethearts who had known each other since age twelve. Only after they were married, and two babies later, did my dad decide he didn't want to be married to my mom anymore. So he dropped my mother, my sister, and me off on my grandparents' door step. But Grandma Stella wasn't one to forgive and forget. After that, she wouldn't let anyone with the last name Lewis near Tina and me. And they hadn't been for nine years. The death of Grandma Stella had opened the door for us to finally meet my dad's family. All of whom, with the exception of my dad, showed up at Grandma Stella's funeral—probably to make sure she was really dead!

As Tina and I looked through the front window of our trailer one morning, we saw Mom talking with a man by the roadside mailboxes. We recognized the man's face. We had seen him around our old neighborhood, visiting his relatives. All the kids called him *Candy Man* or *Uncle Ed* because he always had lots of it and would generously share it with all of us kids.

When we saw him, Tina and I became excited and rushed out of the trailer toward him, screaming for joy at the thought of free candy.

"Hey, Uncle Ed, Uncle Ed... Candy Man! Do you have any candy?"

"Why are you calling him Uncle Ed?" Mom cut in.

"That's what everyone calls him. He's Candy Man," we said, giving her a don't-you-know-that look.

"This is your grandfather!" she said, giving us a don't-you-know-that look right back.

Her words brought the conversation to an abrupt halt as Tina and I stood there looking at her, confused, waiting for the punch line. But it never came.

We looked at Uncle Ed, or—as we had just been informed—Grandpa Ed, for his response. He had been standing there grinning at us the whole time. Then he started to laugh.

Then Mom started to laugh. Tina and I... we weren't laughing. We were still trying to figure out what had just happened.

We clarified.

"So, you're our grandfather?"

"Well, yeah!"

Bending over, he wrapped his arms around us and pulled us in close for a hug. I always thought it strange that Grandpa Ed didn't tell us himself that morning that he was our grandpa. The revelation came instead through our mom.

Coincidentally, or at least Mom said it was a coincidence, Uncle Ed/Candy Man/Grandpa Ed just happened to live directly across the street from us, in a big, pretty, white country house. It sat on a few acres of land and came complete with horses, chickens, cows, and an evil-spirited big dog that seemed to hate the entire world. I had spent many hours staring out the window of our tiny trailer wondering who lived in the big pretty house, wishing so badly to see the inside. Now my wish had come true.

Tina and I took to our new grandpa immediately. After all, we had known him all of our life, well, sort of. After-school time was soon spent at Grandpa Ed's house. His wife, Marge, often spoiled us with her cooking. She was Grandpa Ed's second wife. Grandma Deanny had been his first wife. But Marge was quite the opposite of Grandma Deanny. Marge was White with blond hair and blue eyes. And Mark, the little boy who rode the bus each morning with Starla, was her son. Marge loved to bake and would make us homemade candy apples, caramel apples, cakes, cookies, and mincemeat pie. Plus, she was a great cook—everything she made was delicious.

With Grandpa Ed and Marge across the street, Tina and I were never hungry. Now all we had to do was run across the street. There Marge was waiting to stuff us full of home cooking.

My sister and I enjoyed our new family. And my Aunt Deekay began to spend more nights with her sister, Starla, at Grandpa Ed's house. This gave us all more opportunities for family time. I guess word soon traveled to our dad, Eddie, in Washington, DC, because he joined us for at Grandpa Ed's house for Thanksgiving. As Tina and I sat around the table with Grandpa Ed, Marge, Mom, Aunt Starla and Aunt Deekay, Rodney and Denise, our five-year-old step-uncle Mark, and our prodigal father, Ed Lewis, Jr., I thought about Grandpa Smitty. He was the only person missing and was probably spending Thanksgiving alone. While I was thankful for my new grandpa, I missed my old one.

After only a few months of the country life in Quiet Dell, *we moved again* ...back to town...back to Grandpa Smitty's house. I was so relieved. I had missed him terribly.

The move was bittersweet. I missed being close to Grandpa Ed, my aunts, Starla and Deekay. And I would miss Marge and her cooking. But thankfully, Rodney and Denise were moving with us. Most importantly, my time at Stonewood had mercifully come to an end.

Back in my old neighborhood and old school, I picked up where I left off...I was much happier in my old school, with my old friends.

But my joy was short lived.

I came home from school one afternoon to find Grandpa Smitty lying on the floor in a pool of urine, conscious but unable to stand. He reached for me to help him up, and I tried, but I couldn't. He was too heavy for a ten-year-old. Instinctively, I ran to our neighbor's house and told her to call an ambulance. I ran back to sit with Grandpa Smitty, holding his hand as we waited. Talking on and on about nothing, mostly to keep from being afraid, Grandpa Smitty stared at me in silence. Our neighbor soon joined us. And soon the ambulance came and took Grandpa Smitty away.

Everybody went silent...The same way they did when Grandma Stella went away. Mom refused to talk about it. I begged to visit Grandpa Smitty in the hospital. But my pleas fell on deaf ears. I waited and waited for him to come home.

The news finally came that Grandpa Smitty had died. Once again, my world was shattered. And I cried bitterly. The only father I had ever known was gone. I felt so alone. My ally was gone.

While I had sat through Grandma Stella's funeral quiet, not shedding a tear, Grandpa Smitty's funeral was heartbreaking for me. I missed him terribly.

A year later, Rodney and Denise announced that they were leaving Clarksburg and moving to Los Angeles, California. I had grown close to Rodney and Denise. They had helped fill the void in my life after the death of my grandparents. Now, sadly, they were leaving me too.

With both her parents gone, mom also began making plans to leave West Virginia. She and my nineteen-year-old cousin, Diane, flipped a coin to decide where they would go next...*Head's California...Tails Atlanta*. California won.

Mom asked me if I wanted to join Rodney and Denise in California. Without hesitation, I said yes. I missed my cousins, and I couldn't wait to see them again. After school was out for the summer, Grandma Deanny came to visit me at Diane's house. We sat in the kitchen talking as she made pizza for the two of us, then we sat and ate it together. I had only spent time with her once before that...a whole weekend. Unbeknownst to me, it would be the last time I saw her.

A few days later, Diane and I boarded a Greyhound bus bound for California. Mom promised she and Tina would follow soon and join us in L.A.

Diane and I waved goodbye as the bus pulled out of the station. After we had traveled some miles, we passed a sign that read, *"You Are Now Leaving West Virginia,"* and tears instantly filled my eyes. Reality hit me—I was leaving—I was leaving my newly found family... my childhood friends... my dog, Tody... everything.

I changed my mind. I wanted to go back home. But it was too late.

Chapter Seven: Get Back to Your Roots

A people without the knowledge of their past history, origin, and culture is like a tree without roots.

—Marcus Garvey

Walter Ashby Plecker was a physician and the first Virginia State Registrar of Vital Statistics. He was also a member of *the Anglo-Saxon Clubs of America, the White supremacist organization* that was founded in Richmond, Virginia, in 1922. A devout Presbyterian, Plecker was a staunch supporter of racial purity, the one-drop rule, and segregation. Plecker believed that Negroes living together with Whites would lead to the demoralization of the White race, that Whites were morally, mentally, and intellectually superior to Negroes and that Negroes were incapable of assimilating into White culture.

Jim Crow segregation laws reached their greatest influence from 1910 to 1930. Jim Crow laws held the basic belief that it was unlawful for a Negro and White person to play together or to be in company with each other.[13] Therefore, separate schools were established for Negro children. White children could not attend colored schools, and Negro children could not attend White schools.

I hadn't talked to my grandpa Ed in almost three years, so when I finally called and he answered the phone, I froze. I didn't know what to say, but I knew a good place to start.

"Hey. Granddad!"

"Hey, honey," he answered.

He sounded happy to hear my voice.

I was calling from the girl's dorm at my college. When I told him where I was, he became even more excited. Apparently, he hadn't heard, so this was big news to him.

"I'm so proud of you, girl," he said. "I always knew you were smart. If you get any smarter, I'll have to pay you a dollar every time I talk to you."

His classic West Virginia drawl always made me smile. He was pure country. I loved it.

Trying not to cry, I managed a laugh.

"Thanks, Granddad, but it's really hard. I don't know if I can do it."

"Aww. . . Yes, you can. You hang in there—Don't you quit."

"I won't, Granddad—I won't."

The words stuck in my throat. Granddad's words were few but powerful. And they were just what I needed. I was the only Black student in residence in my college dormitory. In fact, I was the only Black student enrolled in my all-White California private school. Rumor was there was an African student who attended night classes at the college, but I never saw him.

In a matter of weeks, the daily questions from my fellow students, who were eager to ask every question they had ever wanted to ask about Black people, made me realize that I was their bridge to the Black community. By their own admission, they had lived very sheltered lives and hadn't had much, if any, contact with Black people. This was *very* obvious from the comments and questions. Still, as desperate as my White schoolmates were to learn about Black people and the Black culture, I just as desperately wanted to *not* be put on the spot every day. For most of my life, I had been the kid in the background, the kid who just blended in with the walls. Now, being the only Black student at an all-White school made it a little hard to blend.

As I rushed into the dorm one afternoon after class, a boy stopped me in the lobby.

"Hey, can you tell my girlfriend I'm down here waiting for her."

"Sure, what's her name? What room is she in?"

After he told me her name, I said, "Oh yeah, I know her. I'll get her."

"Hey, what's your name?" he added. "I don't think we've met."

"I'm Tracy."

"Where are you from?"

"For the most part, I'm from here, L.A."

"Really. . . You're different. You don't talk Black."

I had turned to run up the stairs until his comment, which made me stop and turn around.

"How are Black people supposed to talk?" I asked, looking at him with a curious look on my face.

"Well, you know what I mean. . . I mean. . ." he stammered, trying to think of something to say.

"Do all White people sound the same?" I asked, cutting in quickly. "Do people from the south sound like people from the north?"

I smiled as I watched illumination dawning in his eyes.

"You know, you're right." He smiled, trying not to look too embarrassed. "I'm sorry about that."

I gave him a forgiving nod. Then I bounded up the stairs to relay the message to his girlfriend.

His comment had caught me a little off guard. I hadn't

heard it from a White person in a long time, not since my Valley school days. Once again, it became a repetitive comment among my new college classmates, who apparently had never been exposed to a Black person, let alone *an articulate* one. I took comfort and pleasure in extinguishing their prejudices one by one as we became better acquainted.

Most memorable college moment number two also happened soon after my arrival. My dorm mate, Cassie, asked as we lounged around the dorm one evening, "Hey, Tracy, can you teach me how to dance?"

Cassie's bright curly red hair and freckles reminded me of the original "Annie" from the Broadway play. On top of that, she was always singing, especially gospel music—her favorites being Aretha Franklin and Sandra Crouch. Cassie and I talked often, so I wasn't insulted by her request. But I was curious.

"What makes you think I can dance?"

I had already anticipated her answer because I had heard the same question from my *Valley* school friends years earlier. Therefore, I was curious to see if her response would be the same as it had the other times.

It was.

"I thought all Black people could dance."

"No, no, that's not true." I said, shaking my head.

I wanted to laugh, but I held back. Cassie looked so perplexed and positively sad with disappointment. Her high hopes of learning how to dance had been dashed. I so badly wanted to tell her the truth—that I was just joking and that I actually could dance. In fact, *I was a very good dancer.* But I was having too much fun dispelling prejudices and extinguishing stereotypes.

I didn't get mad at Cassie. I didn't get mad at people who just honestly had no clue. My Valley school days had showed me that the only way people who lived in a homogenous racial and cultural bubble, like Cassie and my other classmates, would ever learn about Black people and other races was through television and movies, which, unfortunately, were mostly full of stereotypes of minorities and did more harm than good.

I was all too happy to enlighten my classmates. I knew Black history. I knew it well, mostly thanks to growing up with Rodney. However, when it came to my own history, my family, and my life, I was quickly realizing in my all-White college just how much I *didn't* know about my own family...about my own history. As I listened to my dorm mates and classmates share their family stories about their parents and grandparents, going back many years, I grew envious. I was envious of their strong family ties and of how they all knew who they were and where they came from. And I was speechless whenever they asked me questions about my family background, questions about my grandparents, and where I came from. Their questions, once again, reminded me I didn't really know much about my family, especially my dad and his parents.

The questions I had asked as a kid began to echo over and over again in my mind: *What was my history? Where did my grandparents come from? Who were their parents and where did they come from? And why did most of the people in my family have such light skin?*

For years, my inner-city friends had been saying, "You need to get back to your roots!" Therefore, I was finally going to take their advice and *do it*. Reconnecting with Grandpa Ed was my starting point. Taking a break from college, Tina and I decided to take a road trip back east. Tina had moved to California a few years earlier. Shortly afterward, she met and married Marty, a Marine, who was preparing to ship out for six months. They had two little boys, Isaiah, and Isaac, and they would be making the trip with us.

It had been years since I had seen Grandpa Ed, so I was on a mission. I had lots of questions for him to answer. And I had purchased a family tree history book, which I planned to fill in when I saw him.

After Marty shipped out, Tina and I put her furniture and things into storage, then the four of us hit the road. Two weeks later, we arrived in West Virginia, after stopping along the way to visit other family and friends.

As soon as I saw the sign saying, "Welcome to West Virginia" the words "I'm home" crossed my mind. I smiled as I recalled the first time, I had left West Virginia so many years earlier. And as we began to weave our way up and down the curving roads and hills across the Appalachian mountainside, the picturesque mountains brought back memories. I got excited at the thought of seeing childhood friends and family again. While California was my new home, I missed West Virginia; I missed my hometown.

After a few hours, we arrived in Clarksburg. Strangely, the blocks and streets I had once labored to cover the distance of so many times as a kid now seemed so small and narrow. And the library where I often spent hours reading as a child, sitting inside of its big portrait windows was now an old, historical landmark and museum. My hometown had seemed so huge to me as a child. Evidently, years of living in big-city Los Angeles had made my hometown shrink. My grade school, Towers Elementary, and the junior high school still sat there, abandoned, and run down. A town that was once busy and alive now seemed empty and lifeless.

We stopped often along the streets whenever we saw a familiar face walking along. Soon we made our way through town toward the back country roads leading to Granddad's house. There were no signs to mark the roads. One had to be familiar with the usual country road markers that pointed the way to the destination, such as a telephone pole, a white picket fence, a light blue house on the corner, and a bridge—all of which marked the way to his house—all of which Tina thankfully remembered.

Grandma Deanny was gone. She had died shortly after I moved to California. She would be the only person missing on my visit home. Despite the fact that family called me Little Deanny, I had never really gotten to know her before I left for California. We had only met a few times, so I felt cheated.

Turning onto the narrow gravel road leading to Grandpa Ed's house, we made our way down the hill and across the bridge to the road leading up to the house. Grandpa Ed, Marge, Aunt Starla, and Mark were there to greet us as we pulled into the driveway. After the hugs, kisses and greetings, Tina and I put our bags away in the guest room.

I quickly snuggled up next to Grandpa Ed with my genealogy book in hand. I went to work, prying him with question after question as everyone listened and chimed in with their own comments and questions.

Grandpa Ed kept glancing at me, smiling. But I didn't mind. I knew why he stared at me—I was the spitting image of my Grandma Deanny. Besides my dad, I was the only person in our family with brown skin who looked like Grandma Deanny. It wasn't long before Deekay and Starla quickly began calling me Little Deanny again, which made me happy. I stared back at my grandpa in awe of how handsome he was. He had a beautiful, mischievous smile, high cheek bones, and salt-and-pepper hair.

While Grandpa Ed wasn't very good with names, places, or dates, he was a good storyteller and didn't mind sharing stories about his childhood—how his hunting dogs had been his best friends as a boy, how he had delivered a woman's baby in the mountains when he was fifteen years old, and how Big Band music had been his favorite. I took notes excitedly. Grandpa Ed was adding several pieces to the family history puzzle I had been trying to put together—one of the biggest pieces being that his father had been half Italian and half Indian and his mother half Irish. In just a matter of moments his stories, in and of themselves, had answered more than a few of my lifelong questions, chiefly, the skin color question, which had haunted me all of my life.

"You talk White, you need to act Black. You need to get back to your roots," I had been told, over and over by my Black friends over the years.

What if what Grandpa Ed had said was true, that I would never be Black enough for my Black friends...not culturally, not ethnically, and not racially. I had never really gotten away from my roots, but what *were* my roots, exactly? While it was some years before I took their advice, finally—truly—going back to my roots made me understand so much about my family—and about myself.

Chapter Eight: Meet the Family

> A family reunion is a time to remember, a time to laugh, a time to celebrate . . . a time to share old stories and make new memories. A time to see each other in the faces all around us . . .
>
> —Kimberly Rinehart

By 1930, the Census Bureau had reclassified mulatto and White American families as Negro after it was disclosed or became known that the families had *Negro* ancestry in their bloodline--regardless of any other, White, or Indian, ancestry. And despite the fact that many mulattos had married White (some three times over since the early 1800s), *one drop* of Black blood still meant reclassification.

The forced reclassification had a devastating and demoralizing impact on thousands of American families after their multiracial identities were reduced to one—Negro. The establishment and enforcement of miscegenation laws and Jim Crow racial segregation laws came next, setting boundaries for people of color, restricting, and limiting men, women, and children of color socially, professionally, and academically.

In 2006 I sat on the old bridge overlooking the small creek in the backyard of my Grandpa Ed's West Virginia country home, I stared down into the slightly muddy water softly running under the bridge as memories of my hometown came flooding back to me. At the time, I thought my grandfather was the only thing left in Clarksburg to draw me back to the place I had called home for the first twelve years of my life. But I was wrong. Each trip now had a purpose. With each trip I tried to discover more about the family I didn't know. I had been researching my family history for years, trying to find something, anything, to connect me back to the past, back to my ancestors, who (unbeknownst to me) had grown up all around me, in the same town, on the same streets, even right next door to me.

Living in California didn't make it easy. And my work over the years kept taking me further and further away . . . to Alaska, Texas, Tennessee, and Colorado. But now I was in Virginia, trying to connect to my family, trying to find my way back to them through history...through my research.

My attempt to connect had begun in 1997 but had ended quickly, with little success. Taking the bits and pieces of information I had collected from Grandpa Ed in 1991, I exhausted the memories of the family members that I did know. In the end, they would always redirect me to my Aunt Deekay. She was my go-to person for information. But even her knowledge was exhausted by the depth of my many questions. Often, she would refer me to a higher resource—her Aunt Bunch.

"You need to talk to Aunt Bunch. She knows a lot about our family," she would say.

The Aunt Bunch she was referring to was Grandpa Ed's sister—a great-aunt whom I had never met. But according to Deekay, Aunt Bunch held the key to the past—the key to our family history. I knew she was the person I needed to talk to for answers. But she lived somewhere in the mountains of Martinsburg, West Virginia. Thankfully, it was only a few hours away from Clarksburg. Unfortunately, nobody seemed to have her phone number, including Deekay.

When I heard that Aunt Bunch would be coming to Grandpa Ed's 80th birthday party, I got excited and made it a priority to be there. I was looking forward to meeting her. My move to Virginia finally put me closer to West Virginia and closer to Grandpa Ed for the first time in years.

Aunt Bunch was the oldest living matriarch left in the Lewis family. Grandpa Ed was her younger brother and her only living sibling. But they hadn't seen each other in over fifteen years, which was sad seeing as they had only lived four hours from one another for over 50 years, him in Clarksburg, and her on the other side of the mountains, in Martinsburg.

The birthday party was a surprise. And Grandpa Ed was shocked when he saw his sister, Bunch, walk through the door. Lights flashed like crazy all around the event hall as cameras clicked away. Family members shouted for joy as they watched Aunt Bunch and Grandpa Ed laughing as they embraced each other. It was 2006... he was turning 81 and she had just turned 82.

Family members had traveled from Ohio, Michigan, Pennsylvania, Nevada, North Carolina, and Virginia—all the way to Clarksburg to celebrate Grandpa Ed's birthday. I didn't know most of the people at the party, but Tina did because she had grown up on the east coast with our dad. Most of them I had only just met that morning, so I struggled to remember *who was who*. What I did know was this...They were the kids, grandkids, and great-grandkids of Grandpa Ed and Aunt Bunch's brothers and sisters who had long since passed away. Amazingly, most of them had never met Aunt Bunch either. So, I wasn't alone in that.

There had been six siblings—Grandpa Ed and Aunt Bunch were the last two. As the two of them sat side by side at a table on the stage next to a table displaying the pictures of their brothers and sister, and mother and father, they chatted and held hands like little kids. After dinner, I presented them with an 8x10 folder containing several pages of family history, mostly stories I had collected from Grandpa Ed over the years and from the new up and coming website called *ancestry.com*. The few pages were all I had been able to gather up to that point. It wasn't much, but I was very proud of my little booklet. I had put a lot of time and effort into it and had printed out several copies for family members. However, I quickly ran out. I hadn't expected so many people to show up and everyone wanted a copy.

Standing on the stage next to Grandpa Ed and Aunt Bunch, I flipped through the pages one by one, giving my *Lewis Family* presentation. After I finished, I went out to meet and greet some more of my newfound relatives—many of whom were curious and full of questions about my presentation, especially the revelation that great-grandpa Luke was half-Italian.

My meet-and-greet was quickly interrupted by my Aunt Starla.

"Tracy, Aunt Bunch wants you."

Starla pointed to the stage. From across the room, I could see Aunt Bunch motioning for me to come to her. Therefore, I made my way back to the stage. I had been admiring her from afar ever since she arrived but had not yet had a chance to talk with her. She had been crowded by family members the whole time. I knelt down beside her chair, and she put her hand on my shoulder.

With her glasses resting on her nose, she grinned at me, looking very much like a schoolteacher.

"There are a few mistakes in this book," she said, "but you got most of it right."

Aunt Bunch proceeded to flip through the pages of the booklet, articulately commenting on my little project and meticulously pointing out the mistakes here and there. After a few minutes, my knees grew tired. So, I pulled up a chair and sat down next to her, smiling, and taking notes as she turned the pages. Her attention to detail was amazing and impressive. We looked at each other often and laughed. She was witty, articulate, and pensive, pausing every so often to remember a name, or place. And she had a sense of humor and boisterous laugh that made me want to join in.

With her cotton-white hair and pale skin, time had been good to Aunt Bunch. She was still beautiful at 82 years old. Wearing a powder blue pants suit, she looked classy and elegant at 5'4" inches tall.

I stared at my great-aunt in awe, thinking, "Deekay is right. She *is* the one I need to talk to."

As if she was reading my mind, Aunt Bunch turned to me.

"You need to come and visit me in Martinsburg. Then we can go through the papers and photos I have at my home. This is a good start, but honey there's so much more I want to show you."

"I will. I promise. I've wanted to meet you for a long time. I've heard so much about you."

Her invitation thrilled me. I couldn't wait to visit her in

Martinsburg.

Aunt Bunch and I had bonded instantly. She reminded me of myself. It saddened me that we had not met before that day. And when it was time for her to return to Martinsburg, I fought back tears. I didn't want to see her go.

As her car drove away, the words "no fair" echoed in my mind. I felt cheated. She and I had missed a whole lifetime of getting to know each other.

Then a more cheerful thought entered my mind.

"She's not dead, Tracy—you still have time. Go visit her!"

Chapter Nine: A Divine Appointment

Alex Haley told me to go to Warrenton, Virginia, to look for my long-lost relatives, but I didn't do it. I was too scared. I didn't want to go knocking on some White relative's door saying, "Hi! I'm your long-lost relative." I wasn't ready for that.

—Louise "Bunch" King

In 2007, I moved once again—this time to Oklahoma. And my job as a school principal during the day and part-time professor at night put my family research on hold—for a few years. Then I purchased my first home, which sucked up not only my time but also my money—so needless to say, trips to the east and west coast were out.

With my head buried in my work, four years passed quickly. I only saw my east coast and west coast family when they came to me and that was rare. I was truly disconnected and out of touch. As the holidays passed, I missed my family more and more. So feeling the need to reconnect, I dug out my family research papers and scrap books and picked up where I had left off a few years before. My strategy worked. As I searched online through names and websites, I began to feel the connection again.

I called Tina and begged her to track down Aunt Bunch's address for me and she managed to do so. A little nervous but very excited, I wrote to her.

Months passed without a response. Then a few days before Christmas, an envelope from *Louise King* arrived. Enclosed were a letter and a picture and *finally* a phone number, with an encouraging message that said, "Call me."

I anxiously began running through the house looking for my cell phone to dial the number. My heart raced as the phone rang and rang.

Then... she answered.

Her pleasant, proper greeting made me smile. And Aunt Bunch seemed just as happy to hear my voice as I was hers. We had so much to talk about, so we both talked eagerly, on and on for over two hours, sharing stories. Her stories about my Grandpa Ed's "shenanigans" as she called them kept me rolling with laughter. Earlier, it had dawned on me to take notes. I had grabbed a notepad and sat on the floor writing as she talked on and on.

Talking to Aunt Bunch was like talking to Tina, or to my best friend—and just as much fun, if not more. We attempted to end our conversation several times with a goodbye but couldn't. The stories just kept coming. Our personalities were eerily similar, from our personalities and quirks to our likes and dislikes. We were very much kindred spirits, for sure.

I regretted not going to visit Aunt Bunch sooner. I regretted not knowing her sooner. My busy life had gotten in the way, but I decided that night, "no more excuses." Aunt Bunch wasn't going to be around forever. It was now or never. So once again, I promised her I would visit. Then I snared myself with my words by telling her I would come for her 88th birthday in June the following year. I knew if I said it, I would follow through with it.

I kept my promise to Aunt Bunch in June of 2012 and boarded a plane for Washington, DC. Mom met me at Dulles

Airport and the two of us began the drive up the mountain towards Martinsburg to seek out Aunt Bunch. We had barely gotten on the road when I realized I had forgotten my digital recorder in Oklahoma.

"Pull over!" I shouted to mom when I spotted a Walmart sign. "I need a recorder!"

Mom quickly exited the highway and pulled into the parking lot not far from the exit. Jumping out of the car, I ran inside to buy a recorder. I had a very strong feeling I would need one.

On the drive through the mountains to Aunt Bunch's house, I prepped my mother.

"Mom, when Aunt Bunch starts talking, please *do not* interrupt her," I pleaded. "I am going to be recording, so whenever she starts talking, just let her talk. Okay?"

Mom was a marathon talker. She could hijack a conversation in a heartbeat and talk nonstop for hours on end about anything and everything. But in all honesty, if the subject were right, *so could I.*

"Yea, yea, okay," she said.

She acted like it was no big deal. But I knew her better than that—hence, my request.

I had never been to Martinsburg, but it reminded me of any other small, country town hidden in the hills of West Virginia. As we winded our way down one narrow street after another, past rows of side-by-side, weathered, familiar-looking wood-paneled and brick houses, my excitement began to pique. I could hardly wait.

I called Aunt Bunch to let her know we were getting close to her house (per the GPS directions). Then we turned onto a side road just off the main street. At the end of the road was our destination —a two-level, pale green house with a small driveway on the left side. The house had a welcoming country look to it, with tiny windmills, white chairs, and a white-cushioned love seat on the front porch. It was aged like the other homes we had passed, but it seemed sturdy enough. An acre or more of grass rested on either side of the house with a backyard poking out from behind the house and a chain-link fence surrounding the entire property.

The most welcoming feature was Aunt Bunch standing on the front porch, wearing a big smile as she waved a greeting. I bounced in my seat like a little kid anxiously waiting for the car to come to a stop. Once it did, I leaped out of the car and bounded up the stairs, smiling as I hugged my great-aunt. Taking a step back, I breathed a sigh of relief—I had finally made it. I looked around, taking in the view. The still quietness of the small, country road on which the house sat was peaceful and refreshing. The only sound I could hear was my mother's voice in the background as she chatted on about the drive up the mountain.

Staring back at my petite aunt, I was impressed. She had just turned 88 years old but was the picture of health—spry and agile for her age. It was a little hard to believe. But then again, Grandpa Ed was just as spry and healthy, with the exception of his hearing. I had to yell into the phone whenever I talked to him . . . but not Aunt Bunch. She could hear just fine.

Waving us toward the front door, Aunt Bunch beckoned. "Come on, let's go in the house."

"Are you hungry?" she asked as we walked down the hall. "I can start dinner now."

"No, we're fine, Aunt Bunch," I answered.

I was a bit surprised by her offer to cook dinner. She certainly didn't seem helpless in any way, but I didn't want my 88-year-old aunt thinking she had to cook for us.

The three of us walked down the narrow hallway toward the kitchen as Mom talked steadily on about the house, the drive up the mountain, the dogs in the yard, and the cat that met us at the front door. I was distracted by the pictures lining the hallway walls and kept stopping to see if I recognized any of the people in them. But I didn't. They were all strangers to me.

"Aunt Bunch, do you mind later on if I take pictures of your pictures?"

"No, honey, I don't mind." She said, giving me a slightly puzzled. "But how are you gonna do that?"

"With my camera phone," I said, holding up my phone and quickly snapping her picture.

She wrinkled her brow and stood for a moment, looking intrigued—then she glanced to her right at my mother.

"Well, if that don't beat all," she said with a grin. Turning toward the kitchen, she motioned to us with her hand.

"Come on, ladies. It's cool in the kitchen. We can sit around the table."

Mom and I dutifully followed behind her.

The kitchen, with its red brick walls, brown wood cabinets and big black iron stove, had a classic country kitchen look to it. Besides the mixer, microwave, and toaster, it had very few modern conveniences. But it was cozy and cool like Aunt Bunch had said. And it was perfect for hanging out in on a hot summer day.

The back door leading to the back yard opened, and Clarence, Aunt Bunch's handyman, walked in with two big dogs at his heels. The dogs went right to what I assumed were their normal spots on the kitchen floor and laid down. The three of us sat down at the little round table in the middle of the kitchen while Clarence sat on a stool at the counter a couple feet away.

I had just taken my laptop out of my carrying case when Aunt Bunch started in. "You know, I remember when..."

I paused to listen then suddenly remembered my digital recorder. I moved swiftly, digging it out of my bag as Aunt Bunch talked on. I set the recorder on the table and slid it closer to Aunt Bunch, but she didn't seem to notice.

"Do you mind?" I asked, pointing to the recorder.

She stopped talking and looked down at the recorder. Once more, she looked curiously at the little, tiny piece of technology on her table. Again, she wrinkled her brow.

"And what is that?" She asked, peering at me over her glasses with a slight grin.

I quickly explained.

"I figure it'll be easier to record what you say than to try and type it all. This way I can just listen and ask questions. I'll type it all up when I get back to Oklahoma."

She chuckled softly and smiled.

"Oh, honey, that's fine. I don't mind."

I sat listening to Aunt Bunch talk, constantly glancing down at the recorder to make sure it was on. *I didn't want to miss one word.*

Once, Mom interrupted, taking over the conversation with a story of her own. I thought fast, distracting Aunt Bunch with a fake question.

"Hey, Aunt Bunch, who's in that picture over there?"

As soon as Aunt Bunch looked away, I shot Mom a quick... *hey, remember-what-we-talked-about* look, which she didn't miss. She rolled her eyes at me, sighed, and sat back in her chair, yielding the conversation back to Aunt Bunch, who was none the wiser.

Three hours passed like nothing as the four of us sat at the table. The moment felt surreal. I kept telling myself I was actually there, sitting in her kitchen, laughing as Aunt Bunch reminisced about the past, sharing story after story. Clarence laughed along, often nodding and grinning whenever Aunt Bunch looked at him for confirmation.

"Isn't that right, Clarence?"

Mom and I got the feeling Clarence had heard most of these stories many times before, seeing as he had worked for Aunt Bunch for many years.

Taking a break, Aunt Bunch rose from the table, declaring it was time to start dinner. We offered to help her prepare it, but she refused, so we sat and watched.

Mashed potatoes, chicken, and vegetables were the meal *du jour*. As a vegetarian, I picked at the chicken, not wanting to offend my great-aunt. Besides, I was too excited to eat. I had turned off the recorder, thinking the stories had stopped for dinner. But I was wrong. I had to quickly turn it back on when Aunt Bunch picked up where she had left off.

Aunt Bunch was a born storyteller. Listening to her was like listening to an audio book, so I could envision each person and place as if I were there. And her humor was infectious, as was her laughter. She was a natural comedian, and she did not hold back, or tap-dance around the taboo, touchy subjects. Aunt Bunch was a straight shooter, telling it like it was—and she made no apologies. She would often burst into laughter as she reminisced, animatedly using her hands, and slapping her hand down on the table as Mom and I laughed along.

After dinner, the three of us moved to the front porch. I sat next to Aunt Bunch on her wicker love seat while Mom sat nearby in one of the matching white wicker chairs. Several hours had passed since our arrival, but it was still light outside. The West Virginia weather was perfect for sitting outdoors.

Aunt Bunch's house sat near the end of a quiet block. Every now and then a neighbor would wander by and shout out, "Hi, Miss Louise!"

Aunt Bunch would wave back at them with a smile and a polite greeting—then she would turn to us and quietly give us the 4-1-1 on the person.

Around 9:00 PM, Mom retired to bed. Then we, too, called it a night. Clarence had retired to the covered back porch. He would often sleep there in the summertime, with the dogs lying around him.

My body was tired from the drive over the mountain and my mind from the long day of storytelling. But as I lay down on the little twin bed in the spare room, I looked forward to the next day, glad I had come. In just a few hours, I had learned more than I had expected about my family, my great-grandfather, and my great-grandmother. I had never met them. But for a few hours, Aunt Bunch had brought them back to life for me, taking me backwards in time to meet them. I no longer felt like the stranger in my family.

Mom was snoring in the bed next to me. Thankfully, I always carried ear plugs, which I quickly stuffed in my ears. Then I drifted off to sleep . . . happy.

The next morning, I awoke to the sound of the small, metal, old-fashioned air conditioner in the bedroom window laboring hard to blow cool air into the bedroom. Mom's bed was empty. She was an early riser, so I figured she was already downstairs. I quickly jumped out of bed and went searching for mom and Aunt Bunch. Once downstairs, I followed the sound of Mom's voice to the front porch. She and Aunt Bunch were drinking coffee. A sunny and cool country day greeted us once more, so we sat and talked comfortably shaded on the porch. After a few minutes, we made our way back into the kitchen.

When Aunt Bunch started in on another story, I stopped

her. "Hold on... Hold on," I said laughing as I fumbled to turn on my trusty recorder. Aunt Bunch chucked and smiled patiently at me. I smiled back at her, giving her the thumbs-up sign.

"Okay, I'm ready, continue."

I figured Aunt Bunch didn't have a lot of people to talk to besides Clarence, her daughter Serena, and Heather, the home health care worker who came to the house each day. It was clear that she had a lot of stories just waiting to be heard. But she didn't have a lot of people to tell them to. Well, I had waited most of my life to hear them. Because of this, I listened with excitement, letting the recorder do all of the work.

Aunt Bunch got up from the table and walked into the adjoining living room. I could hear her rustling around, talking aloud as she noisily searched for something.

"Do you need any help, Aunt Bunch?" I shouted out to her.

"No honey, I got it," she said returning to the kitchen carrying two, huge old photo albums in her arms. Mom and I moved in closer as she began to pull pictures from the albums. Each picture had a story attached to it—a story Aunt Bunch was quick to tell, once again showing off the sharpness of her mind and impressing us with her amazing attention to detail.

Leaving us with the photo albums, Aunt Bunch again left the room, returning with a folder full of worn, aged papers.

"This is why I wanted you to come. This is what I was telling you about on the phone," she said, handing me the folder.

I laid the folder down on the table and began to flip through the pages slowly and carefully. Each page resembled old parchment paper, so old I thought the pages would tear if I turned them too fast.

As Mom and Aunt Bunch continued to chat and pull pictures from the photo albums, I carefully examined the first page on top of the stack of papers. It was a hand-written letter from a woman named Grace to her cousin, Bunch. I was deeply moved as I read Grace's words to her cousin:

> *All of the 13 original ones have passed and I am the oldest living one in the Grinage family now. They said I have congestive heart failure. My writing is not so good now. I hope you can make it out. The history is incomplete because there are so many new babies I don't know about. What a pity that thru the years we have missed the joy of corresponding and getting to know all of our families. By the way, Joseph Calloway, our cousin, filmed "Roots." They live in California. His mother Harriette is also working hard to get the 'tree' together. I hope you will enjoy all that I've written. My very best to you and your family. Sincerely yours, Cousin Grace.*

I turned to the next page in the stack of aged papers. At the top of the page were written the words: "Cornelia Grayson, born 1849 Warrenton, Virginia." I didn't know that name. It wasn't even remotely familiar to me. Then I realized I was reading the family history journal Aunt Bunch had told me about on the phone. It was the journal Grace had hand-written. As I turned the pages, I noticed it started with the year 1849 and ended with the year 1980. It was detailed, like a bookkeeper's record or any other journal but it included a lengthy family tree with names, birth dates, and marriages, with places and dates, events, deaths, and other significant bits of information about family members and historical figures from the past. I didn't recognize any of the names in the journal. That is, until I came to the year 1919 and read the name, *Louisa Jane Welton O'Banion*. That got my attention...it was a name I knew...it was my great-grandmother, the mother of my Grandpa Ed and Aunt Bunch.

Aunt Bunch cut in on my thoughts when she gently turned

the pages back to page one.

"This is where it all began. Back there in 1849 with Cornelia Grayson—she was my great-grandmother. Grace wrote all of this down a long time ago. She worked so hard on it, for years. And before she died, she made me promise to finish it. I tried to finish it. But I stopped after a while."

Aunt Bunch pushed the journal closer to me. Then she placed my hand on it.

"I have been holding on to this for a long time. When I met you in 2006, I knew right then that you were the one I had been saving it for. It's yours now."

Chapter Ten: Over, Across the Mountain

> Easily one-third of Blacks have White DNA. Why, in light of this, is so much of the focus on tracing ancestry in the Black community and on finding a link back to a region in Africa? In ignoring White ancestry, Blacks are denying their fully articulated multi-racial identities, which developed in America over centuries.
>
> —Debra Dickerson

When I was a teenager, my favorite movies were... *The Godfather* and *Gone with the Wind*. I loved period pieces. They captivated me more than any other type of movie—probably because I was a mental traveler and *a romantic*. I loved traveling around the world in the books I read, and in the movies, I watched, picturing the people and places, and imagining myself there . . . far away from my little country town in West Virginia and far away from the boundaries of my inner-city neighborhood in South Central. My list of "countries to visit when I'm older" was ever expanding...*Scotland, Italy, Austria, Australia, Spain* and more.

The thought of being whisked away to another country, place, and time made me dwell on the past, on how things used to be and how people used to live. Inevitably, I would start thinking about my own family, about my parents, about the grandparents I barely knew, and about the great-grandparents I never knew. Then the questions would start all over again...

"Where did I come from? Who were my ancestors? What were their names? Where did they come from?"

Alex Haley had charged my great-Aunt Bunch with the task of crossing over the mountain to search for her long-lost relatives. But she never did it—the fear of rejection had dissuaded her. Thirty years had passed since that charge. The time had finally come to cross over the mountain. Yet, instead of Aunt Bunch making the journey, it was me. And I couldn't wait. Warrenton, Virginia, was the starting place. Just across the state line, not far from Aunt Bunch's home, was the birthplace of my great-great-great-grandmother, Cornelia Grayson.

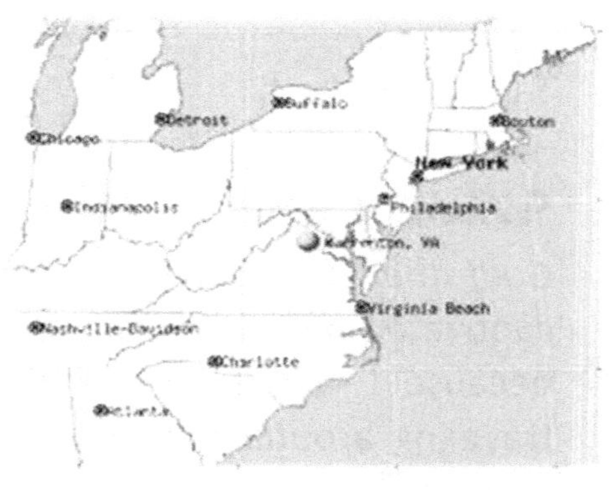

Enlisting the help of Vickie, the Warrenton Library genealogist, we searched through the Warrenton Library archives, through pages and pages of seemingly endless historical records and documents. Then after months and months of searching, a door to the past finally opened up. Vickie called me excited. She had found what I was looking for. And as I stared at the pages from the Fauquier County ledger, once again tears filled my eyes, just as they had when I first discovered Great-Grandpa Luke.

Through the tears, I could read the name of my great-great-great-grandmother. . . The name Cousin Grace had written so many years earlier in her journal—Cornelia Grayson. I smiled. Then I began to laugh. I had found the woman I had been hearing about in Bunch's stories and reading about in the pages of Cousin Grace's family history journal.

I couldn't wait to call Aunt Bunch. We talked often. I

shared every little discovery and revelation with her so that she could make the journey with me as I uncovered more and more of our family history. Now I could tell her that I had found her great-grandmother, Cornelia Grayson, born in Warrenton, Virginia...but in 1834, not 1849. But our history didn't start there. The more I searched the more I discovered.

The story goes...

Benjamin Grayson was born circa 1684 in Dumfries, Scotland. A Scottish merchant, he left his home of Dumfries for the colonies around 1715. After landing on the shore of Westmoreland County, Virginia, he set out to build a new life for himself in a new country with nothing but an ax in his hand. Settling in Prince William County Virginia, Benjamin Grayson was one of the first merchants to settle on Quantico Creek. Determined, opportunistic, and driven, he traded in tobacco and dry goods, supplying crackers, biscuits, and wheat bread to colonists and sea vessels trading along the shores of the Occoquan Bay. His popularity in social circles and among politicians grew quickly. And he became known for having a good head for business. He acquired great wealth as a result of his baked goods and tobacco-trading businesses.[14]

Benjamin Grayson soon married Susanna Monroe (the aunt of President James Monroe). The two built a plantation home facing the Potomac, which they named Belle Aire. It was situated on the southeast corner of Prince William County, Virginia, with South Colchester two miles to the East and Occoquan Mills three miles to the north. The couple had four children: Benjamin II, Spence, William, and Susanna.[15]

At the age of fifty-seven, Benjamin Grayson, Sr., died at his home in Belle Aire. The Grayson children continued their father's business and political success, branching out into

Kentucky and Pennsylvania. Benjamin Grayson, II, expanded his father's baked goods business into new ventures, including the establishment of a flour-mill, a bakery, and a dry goods store. He fathered three sons—Frederick William Spence, John, and Alfred. (Repetitive names were tradition among Scottish clans. It enabled them to keep track of and trace their lineage and ancestry.)

In Virginia, slaves were a necessary commodity for any wealthy southern family in the 1700s and 1800s. And the Graysons were no exception. The more slaves one held, the higher one's stature in the community was elevated. The Grayson estates and plantations were some of the finest in all of Virginia. And the plantations included nearby cabins for the slaves. By 1778, the state had forbidden the importation of slaves into Virginia. Despite this, the birth rate among slaves continued to increase at a rapid pace,[16] as slaves constituted over forty percent of the population of Virginia.[17]

Cornelia Grayson

The following is based on family history documents from archived records, library genealogy records, vital statistics death and marriage records, county registry documents, and on a family history journal written by my great-cousin, Grace Grinage-Pride, which she passed on to her great-cousin, my Aunt Louise "Bunch" King.

Cornelia Grayson was born in 1834 in Warrenton, Virginia, the daughter of a Scottish plantation owner and a mulatto mother. Birth and death records were not recorded with the county registry until 1849. Families usually recorded such events in family Bibles, in family history journals, and in ledgers. This changed in 1849 as all persons in Fauquier County were required to register with the county to declare their status as White, free-born, slave, or freed-slave. It was at that time that plantation owner Frederick William Spence Grayson registered his fifteen-year-old daughter, Cornelia Grayson, in the registry—listing his name alongside hers. Also written next to Cornelia's name in the registry were the words free-born, a term that was only ascribed to a handful of people in the registry containing hundreds of names.

Born on the Grayson plantation, Cornelia was pretty and petite at 5'2" with pale skin, thin wavy black hair, and dark brown eyes. She was mulatto. But her pale bright skin caused many people to assume her *simply White*—that is, people who didn't know her. She had inherited her father's defining Scottish features and bore a striking resemblance to her great-aunt, Eliza Grayson, who was also described as having dark curly hair, *dark brown expressive eyes*, and pale clear skin. Cornelia spent most of her time baking and cooking in the plantation kitchen. Baking was a craft the Grayson family had perfected—that and politics. The two had made the Graysons very wealthy and very influential.

While her free-born status and White features afforded her some privilege, there were limitations. She was still a mulatto, therefore, not fully White. So therefore, she was not allowed to learn to read or write. Virginia law strictly forbade anyone other than Whites to learn how to read and write. And the penalty for breaking the law was thirty-nine lashes with a whip, plus a fine.

Cornelia could come and go as she pleased to and from the plantation. However, even free-born mulattos, as well as freed slaves, were in constant danger of being captured and resold, or subjected to acts of cruelty. The continual threat of torture, kidnapping, and death were a constant reminder of how little the word free meant to a free-born person in Virginia.

Slave hunters often captured free-born mulattos and sold them into slavery in other states. Slave hunters knew that, if captured, free-born persons could not defend themselves. Only Whites possessed rights. And in Virginia, only Whites could speak out against other Whites and defend themselves inside a courtroom. A mulatto or a Negro could be shot and killed by a White person, on the spot, for even the slightest offense. And the White person would not suffer any judgment. Thus was the law and culture of 1849 Virginia.

Moreover, Virginia law stated that any person who was declared free could only remain in the state for one year after being declared free. So, in 1850, one year after being registered as a free-born mulatto, Cornelia prepared to leave Virginia. Slave owners did not want to risk free-born persons or freed slaves influencing and encouraging bonded slaves to run away or to rise up and rebel against their slave owners. But if a free-born person or a freed slave wished to remain in the state beyond the one-year limit, then he or she needed to obtain written permission to do so.

Cornelia could have easily stayed in Virginia. But her family had made other plans for her. An arranged marriage was awaiting her in Pennsylvania. Plantation families were close in their associations. So were their servants and slaves. And plantation families often visited one another to arrange marriages between their families and their slaves. In the 1800s, class systems existed even among free-born mulatto families, who would often arrange for their children to intermarry with other free-born persons in other counties and states.

The Grayson plantation had a pretty wide reach socially and economically. Their plantations covered thousands of acres and their business dealings and influence stretched from the Blue Ridge Mountains of Virginia up and over into Pennsylvania, down into Kentucky and even into the southern states. The Graysons held close ties to other family members who owned plantations across the south and along the east coast.

In 1850, there were no paved roads through the mountains. A journey to Pennsylvania could take up to a month, or even longer. But leaving behind her home, her friends, and her family, Cornelia began the tiresome, arduous, and dangerous journey from Virginia, traveling by horse, wagon, and by ferry to begin her new life in Pennsylvania.

Fifteen years later, in 1865, after the end of the Civil War, Virginia records record that Frederick William Spence Grayson freed all of his slaves. He died a year later in 1866.

Chapter Eleven: Sylvester, the Shoemaker

Grace started the family history with Cornelia because that's where it all started. That's why Alex Haley said our family went from White to Black. My great-grandparents were mostly White. They both looked White, and their children looked White. They were proud of who they were. They had thirteen children—some of them married White in between, including my grandmother Sarah.

—Louise "Bunch" King

Years ago, in the early 1800s, a culture existed that was frowned on and despised *by the southern states*—a culture that championed freedom and equality for all men. The first and greatest of the abolition societies were founded in Pennsylvania and it was there that the first law to bring slavery to an end was passed. Probably owning more Negroes than any other people in the colonies, *the Quakers* were, without a doubt, the principal slave-holders in Pennsylvania. However, in 1665 William Edmundson asked his fellow Quakers this question— *"How is it possible to reconcile with Christ's teaching the practice of holding slaves without providing them with the hope or expectation of freedom?"* [18]

A crisis of conscience continued into 1688 as Pastorius and three associates, all of them German Quakers who had recently come to Pennsylvania and settled at Germantown, issued a memorable protest against slavery, again, asking the simple questions: *"Would the masters wish so to be treated?"* And, *"How could Christian people do such things?"*

Pastorius's questions ignited conscientious conviction throughout the Quaker society. So much so that, by 1778, there was widespread sentiment favoring legislative abolition of slavery. The Abolitionists' opposition of slavery gradually became more intense until, at last, on March 1, 1780, the bill was enacted into a law. Thus, Pennsylvania became the first state to pass a law to abolish slavery.[19]

It was into this brave abolitionist society, with its diverse culture and practices, that my great-great-great-grandmother, Cornelia Grayson, was deposited upon her arrival from Virginia. Southwestern Pennsylvania was in every way *different* from the world she had left behind in Virginia. In Virginia, she had been a free-born mulatto girl with pale, bright skin—not a slave, but not truly free. While she had been free-born, only written permission and an escort had allowed her to leave the plantation boundaries of her Virginia home. In Pennsylvania, however, those boundaries disappeared.

In Pennsylvania, a whole new world opened up for Cornelia. In Cornelia's new world, her strong Scottish features caused people to respond to her as White. She could come and go whenever and wherever she pleased, without the need for permission and without fear. For the first time in her life, she felt truly free.

An arranged marriage had awaited Cornelia in Pennsylvania. Soon she would marry Sylvester—a man she had never met. But he had been chosen as a suitable husband for her by her family. With her future and destiny arranged, she prepared to marry.

My great-great-great-grandfather, Sylvester Finley Grinage,

was born in 1826 in Pittsburgh, Pennsylvania. Friends had given him the nickname, *the Shoemaker,* because he made shoes for a living. The son of a Dutch father and a mulatto mother, Sylvester had inherited his father's surname and his Scandinavian features. His father had also been a plantation owner. But by the time Sylvester was born, slavery had already been abolished in the state of Pennsylvania. Therefore, he had never known slavery—only freedom.

At the age of twenty-four, Sylvester was handsome, ambitious, and educated—*he could read, write, and do arithmetic*. But he was a shoemaker by trade—one of the best in the city of Pittsburgh. Every day he went to work in his little shoe shop in the bustling business district of Pittsburgh's famous Townsend Street and Wylie Avenue, making shoes for his customers, which included some of Pittsburgh's wealthiest families. He was proud of his little shoe shop...And business was very good.

Anxious for him to settle down and begin a family, Sylvester's family made plans for him to marry Cornelia Grayson, a pretty, free-born mulatto girl from the Grayson Plantation in Virginia. At sixteen, Cornelia was of marrying age, so, through the grapevine plantation network, letters were sent, and the arrangements were made for Cornelia to join Sylvester in Pennsylvania.

Six months after Cornelia's arrival in Pennsylvania, the two were married. The couple moved to Monongahela City to settle down closer to Sylvester's shop in Pittsburgh. Originally called Parkinson's Ferry, Monongahela City was the oldest settlement in Pennsylvania's Monongahela Valley. The ferries on opposite sides of the river of the same name conducted most of the river traffic in the area.[20] The river also teemed with fishing boats, which moved back and forth, in between the visiting steamboats. Each morning, Sylvester traveled the sixteen miles by horseback and by ferry between his home and work.

While Sylvester worked at the shoe shop, Cornelia also worked, doing what she did best—*baking*. Cornelia loved to bake and had done a lot of it at her plantation home in Virginia. Baking was a craft that ran in the Grayson family. Benjamin Grayson, Sr., had brought the craft with him from Scotland, years earlier, in the late 1700s. The family's baked goods business had made the Grayson's very wealthy... So, Cornelia followed suit by running her own business right out of her home.

Word spread quickly. In no time at all, Cornelia's breads, especially her gingerbread, made her well known around town and around the city. Great-Cousin Grace would later write in her journal: "People would come from all over the city to buy her breads and cakes."

A year after their wedding, Cornelia and Sylvester welcomed their first child, William. The flood gates opened, and the family began growing by leaps and bounds as twelve more children followed, in succession, plus two adopted children—Sarah Jane, Susanna, Benjamin, Isabella, Eliza Jane, Beverly, Lincoln, Sadie, Sylvester Jr., Cora, Melissa, Joseph, Abraham, and Mary. Sylvester and Cornelia loved their large clan. And together they worked hard to make a good life for their children.

Among her children and husband, Cornelia was the only one who could *not* read and write. She had never been afforded the opportunity in Virginia because of her *mulatto* status. Not being *fully* White, she was denied the privilege of learning to read. Therefore, she took great pleasure in watching her children learn how to read and write. And education became the top priority in the Grinage home. Hard work became priority number two.

Pennsylvania in the mid-1800s was exceptionally different from the rest of the states, especially the southern states. In Pennsylvania, a person's race was determined by their skin color and features. If a person looked White, then they were considered White... if a person looked Negro, then they were considered Negro, or colored. Another radical difference was that mulattos could freely intermarry with other Whites. In Pennsylvania, at that time, there were no laws prohibiting interracial marriage.

American historian Edward Turner wrote:

> *In 1726 intermarriage with White people was forbidden in the strongest possible manner. By the same act Negroes were not allowed to meet together, and were subjected to a number of minor restrictions. All of these regulations affected free Negroes as well as slaves. By the act of 1780 they were swept aside. Negroes were now put nearly upon a plane of equality with White persons.*[21]

Interracial marriage among mulattos and Whites was all too common in Pennsylvania in the 1800s. However, in 1830 there arose a minority of White citizens who objected to the number of interracial marriages taking place in Pennsylvania, believing that Negroes were seducing minor White children into marriage.[22] Protestors petitioned the county and asked that interracial marriages "be made an offence against the laws of the State."[23] Despite the freedom and equality culture preached by the outnumbering abolitionists, the protestors' petition resulted in fewer and fewer interracial marriages being performed.

By 1915, twenty-eight states had declared marriages between Negroes and White persons unacceptable, with six states including this prohibition in their constitutions.[24]

Chapter Twelve: Dreamers and Shakers

Every great dream begins with a dreamer. Always remember, you have within you the strength, the patience, and the passion to reach for the stars to change the world.
—Harriet Tubman, Escaped Slave, American Activist

A recent internet discussion between parents on children raising children ignited a heated debate. Several moms attacked the issue *and* each other. Almost all of the moms agreed that having children help raise their brothers and sisters was wrong and that children should not be expected to do anything more than take out the trash, wash the dishes, and make their beds.

First mom: "When children are adults then they can have all the responsibilities of a parent. It's not a child's job to care for their siblings; it's their parents' job, period!"

Second mom: "Kids should be able to hang out with other kids, play sports, and have time to read, or listen to their music. It's the parents' job to care for siblings."

Thus was the consensus of opinion and the repeated sentiments of each chatroom mom, that is, until one mom dared to disagree. She told how she used household chores to build character in her kids, and how her kids often helped her around the house by changing the baby's diapers, cooking meals, washing dishes, taking out the trash, mopping the floors, and cleaning their own rooms. Her post started a frenzy among the other chat room moms, who began a verbal assault on the mom and refused to listen to anything else she had to say.

The actions of the chat room moms both surprised and amused me.

"My, how times have changed," I said out loud.

Then I sighed as I thought of my sister, Tina, who, at age ten, had taken on many of the caretaker duties after the death of our grandparents. Tina had often sat at my grandmother's side, carefully watching, and helping her prepare dinner each night. Tina could fry chicken, make spaghetti, hot dogs, hamburgers, meatloaf, mashed potatoes, *and gravy*—pretty much anything Grandma Stella cooked. Tina loved to cook...And for this I was grateful. Her skills came in handy after Grandma Stella died because we were often left alone to care for ourselves. Many times, we had gone to bed hungry...not starving, but hungry. Because food was at times scarce in our home, we would often raid some of the neighborhood gardens for vegetables. Other times, the Girl Scout's brought bags of groceries to our door. Tina was good at creating something to eat out of very little. My favorite dish was her *spaghetti noodles in Campbell's tomato soup sauce.*

Cora and Eliza Jane

At the age of forty-two, after bringing thirteen children into the world, and adopting two more, Cornelia Grayson's world came to an end. She died suddenly, leaving Sylvester a widower with several small children to raise. Their two oldest children, William, and Anna, had married early on and had left home, leaving thirteen children at home. Therefore, the responsibility of raising the rest of the children fell to the next oldest daughter, my great-great-grandmother, Sarah, who was only eighteen when her mother died. While mostly unheard of in the 21st century, in 1878 it was customary for the oldest child to take over the caretaker responsibilities for his or her brothers and sisters after the death of a parent.

Sarah had large shoes to fill. But she filled them quite well. She accepted her role as homemaker, continuing her mother's baking business, a task she also did quite naturally. Everyone looked up to Sarah. She could cook and clean *and* read and write. Like Tina, she had paid close attention at her mother's side for 18 years., which made her more than capable of raising her brothers and sisters.

Sylvester Sr., meanwhile, was still the principal wage earner for the family. He continued to work at his shoe shop. The Civil War had raged all around Pennsylvania, consuming and depleting much of the state's resources. But in 1878, reparations and restorations were being made all around the city of Pittsburgh. The coal mines and steel factories were booming, and Pennsylvania was growing again. It was now home to some of the wealthiest families in America, such as the Melons, the Carnegies, and *the Thaws*.

Cora Grinage was fifteen years old when her mother, Cornelia, died. With tough times ahead, the oldest of the Grinage kids all pitched in to help, except for Cora. The family agreed that Cora should stay in school. Cora was gifted. She loved to learn, and she was a diligent student. Cora stood out among the other students at her school. She made her teachers and her parents proud. Her father, Sylvester, would often brag about his children to his friends and clients, especially Cora, his overachieving daughter.

Cora's love for learning and her constant service at her church brought her great praise and kind words from everyone who knew her. She often volunteered in and around the community, whenever and for whatever cause presented itself. Cora's hard work did not go unrewarded. She soon caught the attention of one of the wealthiest women in Pittsburgh, Elizabeth Thaw.

Elizabeth Thaw was the wife of William Thaw, II. The Thaw family was known for its generosity and benevolence. And they were the most prominent of Pennsylvania's wealthiest, aristocratic families. The family's Allegheny home was a large and lavish one. They were known to keep at least nine household servants at all times, including two nursemaids, a cook, a housekeeper, a waiter, and a coachman. Fervent Presbyterians, the Thaws attended Third Presbyterian Church, a church that Cora often visited and volunteered at. Becoming Cora's benefactress, Mrs. Elizabeth Thaw offered to pay for Cora to attend college. Her generosity led to Cora becoming the first of her Grinage clan to attend college.

Cora chose William Wilberforce University, a private school named in honor of 18th century British abolitionist, William Wilberforce. Started in 1856, the school was a destination point for the Underground Railroad. It had met with early success until the Civil War forced it to close due to dwindling financial support. After the Civil War, the University was reopened in 1887. After its reopening, Cora enrolled and worked hard to make not only her mother and father and brothers and sisters proud but also her benefactress, Mrs.

Elizabeth Thaw.

Cornelia's daughter, Eliza Jane Grinage, named after her grandfather's sister, was the mother of my great-cousin Grace Grinage-Pride, who wrote in her journal about her mother's main passion in life. An activist in the support of women's rights, Eliza Jane made her own special mark in her town and on the city of Pittsburgh. Bold, confident, and outspoken, women's rights, according to Grace, became Eliza Jane's calling. And she steadily championed the movement alongside her sister-in-law, Nancy.

Nancy worked as a housekeeper for Lillian Russell—an actress, opera singer, and star of the stage and theatre. Lillian was Pittsburgh's *and the world's* most famous celebrities. Later in life, Lillian would become a close friend and companion of actor W. C. Fields. But in Eliza Jane's time, Lillian was best known around Pennsylvania as an outspoken leader in the push for women's rights in Pennsylvania. Nancy would often recruit Eliza Jane to help her prepare for Lillian's marches and rallies.

In 1897, Eliza Jane did her part for the city of Pittsburgh by organizing the first *Women's Day* celebration in the city. For her effort, she won a remarkable $35 (roughly equal to $500 today). It also earned her a picture in the local paper. Her daughter Grace was only one year old at the time, but she later wrote about her mother's achievements in her journal. Grace's cousin, Louisa "*Bunch*" King would also recall the event later in life.

When I was living in Winchester, Virginia, I went to a church service and a lady got up in the church and said, "I want to introduce someone. All these years we have had a celebrity in our midst." Then she said my name. When she did, I thought, "Are you crazy?" She went on to talk about Eliza Jane, my grandmother's sister and how she had founded Women's Day in 1897 in Pittsburgh, Pennsylvania. I had written an article about it, but I was surprised when this woman called me out in church. The article is still around here somewhere in some of my papers.

Historical documents and records from the late 1800s classified Sarah and her brothers and sisters as White. Because of this, they were afforded the same freedom, advantages, and opportunities as any other White family living in Pennsylvania. Therefore, Eliza Jane and Cora knew no boundaries...Pennsylvania society made it easy for them to move through life and into careers unhindered by the restraints of color and status. In Pennsylvania, there were no limits...all doors were open to them.

Sylvester continued to make shoes in his shoe shop until his death in 1896. Having never left the state of Pennsylvania, the hard-working father of fifteen was buried next to his beloved Cornelia. His spirited work ethic greatly influenced his children to never give up and to never quit. He and Cornelia's entrepreneurial spirit had paved a way for their children and set a standard they worked hard to live up to.

While it was common for girls to marry young in the late 19th century, my great-great-grandmother, Sarah, had waited. At eighteen, her life was busy and full—busy raising and providing for her twelve younger brothers and sisters after the death of their mother. But finally, after her work was done...after seeing all of her siblings married and settled into lives of their own, Sarah's turn finally came. It came in the form of *William O'Banion*, whom Sarah had known for some time. Her older brother, William, had married William O'Banion's cousin, Elizabeth, several years earlier. So, in 1890, at the age of thirty-two, Sarah and William married. Eleven years after they were married, Sarah and William welcomed a baby girl into the world...my great-grandmother, Louisa Jane Welton O'Banion. Louisa would be William and Sarah's only child. They later adopted a niece, Olive, who was six years older than Louisa.

The two became very close.

Sarah's life ended in 1918. At the age of sixty-two, she too died of congestive heart failure, the same illness that had claimed her mother, Cornelia. The same illness that would later claim the life of Cousin Grace.

William never remarried after Sarah's death. He took Louisa and moved to the coal mining town of Hempfield in Westmoreland, Pennsylvania. There, he met an Italian-Indian coal miner named Luke Louis. William introduced Luke to his daughter Louisa, who was instantly smitten with the handsome, rugged man. Less than a year later, at the age of seventeen, Louisa married the much older, thirty-two-year-old Luke Louis, and the two began married life under her father's roof in Westmoreland.

Chapter Thirteen: Family Skeletons

> They called my dad Geechi. My father let the grandchildren call him that. But he didn't like it. And nobody else would dare call him that. He wouldn't have it. Geechi's were Black people from the south who looked White, so people would just call 'em Geechi.
>
> —Louise "Bunch" King

Why did America abolish slavery in 1865 but not segregation? Because...while a change in the law could outlaw and prohibit slavery, it could not change the minds, morals, and prejudices of many White Americans, who continued to view people of color (Blacks, Indians, Asians, and Latinos/Hispanics) as inferior and unequal. Therefore, segregation was *a safeguard* that America used to keep people of color separate from Whites. It was a means of keeping people of color *in their place*, so to speak...the place America had assigned to them, the place *beneath* that of White America.

Socially, academically, and professionally, segregation limited people of color and told them where they could and could not go, sit, eat, and study. Moreover, segregation came in handy when it came to work, seeing as it restricted the types of jobs people of color could hold in America.

My great-grandfather, *Luke Louis*, was born in Alabama, to an

Italian father and a Cheyenne Black-Seminole mother. Black Seminoles were the descendants of the "Gullah" people of Florida. Gullah were known for speaking a language referred to as "Geechi." The Gullah had lived side by side with refugee Seminole Indians, often intermarrying (*Seminole comes from the Spanish word, "Cimarron," meaning runaway, or hidden away*).

However, it was not Great-Grandpa Luke's Cheyenne Seminole blood that was an issue...it was the one-eighth portion of Black blood (as if it could be quantified) flowing through his veins that subjected him to Alabama's one-drop rule and the strict segregation and discrimination laws that came with the one-drop rule.

After his parents and brothers and sister left Alabama in the early 1900s and moved to Pennsylvania, Great-Grandpa Luke found it hard to remain in the south, so he too decided to migrate north. There, the stories of the freedom culture and unsegregated world of Pennsylvania, as opposed to the segregation and discriminating culture of the south, proved to be everything he had heard about. There he found *not only work* but also freedom—freedom from the segregation and discrimination he had been surrounded by and subjected to in the South.

Standing at her kitchen table holding a bowl of mashed potatoes, Aunt Bunch was laughing. She had been steadily chatting on as she whipped the mashed potatoes by hand. She was preparing dinner for Mom and me, refusing our help. I felt a little guilty letting my eighty-eight-year-old Aunt do all the cooking, but she was adamant about it, and stubborn.

Looking at the clock on the wall, I realized the three of us had been sitting around the kitchen table for hours talking and laughing as Aunt Bunch shared story after story. I hadn't even noticed the time. I was having too much fun listening to her reminiscence about the past. Her wry wit only added to the enjoyment as she talked animatedly with her hands, laughing at her own stories.

It had been a long time since I had laughed so hard and smiled so much. My mom seemed to be having just as much fun, and she was unintentionally proving to be a good interview partner. As Aunt Bunch talked, Mom would ask who, what, when, and where questions, which would cause Aunt Bunch to go even deeper into the story. And all I had to do was just sit and listen.

Aunt Bunch's face suddenly turned serious as she laid the bowl of potatoes down on the table.

"Our family has a few skeletons," she said with a serious look on her face.

Mom and I listened closely.

She continued. "You know it used to be, the worst thing a person could have in their family was a horse thief. But not our family—we had worse!"

Slapping the table with her hand and bursting into laughter, her serious tone quickly switched to humorous as Mom and I laughed along with her.

I was eager to hear about the skeletons, so I quickly glanced down at my recorder, sat cross-legged in the chair, and leaned with my elbows resting on the table, listening closely as Aunt Bunch continued.

The following story is Aunt Bunch's story in her own words.

Rumor had it that my dad had been married once before—that he had twin daughters from that marriage. {Alabama records show Alabama as Luke Louis' birthplace. They also record that he was never married to Sophie Brown—but he was the father of her children}

But my dad never talked about it. He never really talked much about what happened to him in Mississippi before he met my mother. Mississippi was always a great big mystery to us. We weren't ever allowed to ask him about it. Now my sister Martha, she was good at getting my dad to talk. Sometimes she could get answers out of him.

Up until we left Pennsylvania around 1931, my father worked as a coal miner in Westmoreland, Pennsylvania. That's where we were all born. My brother William was born first, then my sister Martha. The rest of us followed one by one—Franklyn, Robert, me, then Ed, and Sarah was born last. But Sarah didn't stay with us long. We lost her to death shortly after her first birthday.

My grandmother Josephine lived with us in Pennsylvania when I was around five years old. My uncle's wife, Willa-Nita also lived with us. She was Indian, too, like my grandmother. Willa-Nita was married to one of my dad's brothers—to my dad's brother Gartha I think. But I can't say for sure. My dad had another brother, but we didn't see him around much. And I don't remember his name. His brother Gartha I remember because he came around a lot. He was a bootlegger, and he always carried a gun, which he didn't hesitate to use. He had a reputation for being a pretty bad character. But he was good to us kids. He would play the guitar for us and sing. My dad liked to sing, too. So we'd all sit around singing while Gartha played the guitar. Our family, we all got along pretty well.

I never knew my dad's father's name until today when you told it to me—Blainey. Nobody ever knew his name—not even my older brothers and sisters. We had never seen him, never met him. My father never talked about him, never even spoke his name. And we were forbidden to ask about him. My mother made that clear. So we would speak in whispers about him. Whenever we brought up the subject of dad's father around our mother, she'd snap at us, "Never ask your daddy about your grandfather!"

Back then if you wanted to find out anything, you had to eavesdrop 'cause grownups wouldn't tell you nothing if you were a kid.

My dad and Uncle Gartha had an older sister, Georgia, but they called her Georgey. She didn't have the same father as my dad and Gartha. She was their half-sister. But they all had the same mother. They all looked alike—White—but Gartha looked Italian, just like my dad.

People were scared of Uncle Gartha, especially my mother. She was scared to death of Gartha. But she never would tell us why. Then one day, someone came and told my dad that Gartha was dead. What happened was, he went outside one night to the outhouse to use the bathroom, and the gun he was carrying fell out of his pants and shot him to death.

Now that's the one story your granddaddy actually got right.

Long after Gartha had shot himself to death, when I was a teenager, I was sitting talking to my mother, and I asked her, "Why were you so scared of Uncle Gartha?"

She said, "Well, you're older now and he's gone, so I guess it won't hurt to tell you."

My grandfather, this Blainey fellow, was awfully mean to my grandmother. He used to torment her and beat on her so much it was driving her crazy—nuts. The poor woman couldn't take it anymore—she started losing her mind. On top of that, my grandfather, Blainey, was deep into black magic and witchcraft. And he was always mixing up potions and other mess, trying to put spells on people.

Well, Gartha and my dad finally decided they were going to put a stop to him. They were tired of him treating their mom so bad. But they didn't know how to stop him. So they started conspiring and came up with a plan. They decided to use his black magic against him. So they went to this fortune teller to learn how to make a voodoo doll. They wanted to cast a spell on him. Even though my father and Gartha had grown up around witchcraft and black magic, they didn't know how to use it. But the fortuneteller, she told them where to go to find all the stuff they needed to make the voodoo doll.

She told them, "When you finish, everything will be

okay, and your mother won't act crazy anymore."

Well, they did what she said. They went out and found it all—the hair, the pins, and the other stuff they needed to make the doll. Then they burned whatever they could find that belonged to the man, believing that would do the trick and take care of him.

But it didn't work—not even a little bit. After all that, the father was still just as nasty and mean, if not more. So then they got desperate, or at least Gartha did. One night Gartha and some of his friends, some of the men he ran around with, they drove up to his father's house one night and took him out of his bed. They shoved him in the car, drove out to the coal fields, and drug him up onto one of those hilltops where the coke ovens were burning hot, white hot. And Gartha shoved his father into one of those coke ovens—alive. Then he slid the door shut. Now those coke ovens burned all day long. So when he shoved the man into that coke oven, it was all over.

I don't know if my dad was there or not that night. My mother never said he was, but you know, I've often thought about this... Somebody who was there had to come back and tell my mother the story. And I doubt it was Gartha. My parents definitely knew about it. Gartha threatened to kill my mother if she ever told anyone. And she believed he would have done it because he could be mean—mean just like his daddy. So my mother was scared to death of him. That's why she never told a soul for years, not until after the gun fell out of his pants and shot that fool.

My grandfather . . . Blainey Louis . . . he was the one who died in that oven that night. Nobody probably ever even missed the man.

After my mother told me what happened, then I understood why my father never spoke my grandfather's name. And I thought about my poor grandmother living with that crazy man, being so mistreated. People didn't do anything about women being beaten and abused back then. They knew about it, but they just said, "Oh, she's just a woman." Well, I tell you what—she didn't get any more beatings after that.

My oldest brother's name was William Bloomy Louis. And I always wondered where my father got such a strange name from—Bloomy. Now you made me wonder if his middle name was supposed to be Blainey, after our grandfather.

[I wondered too, so I did a quick internet search of the origin of the name Bloomy. The search defaulted to one name, Blaney or Blanee—the name of *my* great-great-grandfather, and *Bunch's grandfather*, whom she had never met. Like many Americans back then, great-grandpa Luke Louis could barely read and write. Words and names were written according to the way they sounded—hence the name *Bloomy* instead of *Blainey*.]

There were a lot of those coke ovens there along the hills

in the back fields in our town. You could see them burning from out your back windows way back up on the hills. My father worked up there around those ovens. When I was a girl, I had nightmares about those coke ovens for years, but nobody believed me.

In my dream each night, I would start off running through this field. Then I would go running along this long row of coke ovens that sat on a hill. As I ran, these coke ovens would shoot fire up behind me. Now remember, those ovens were white hot. And in my dream, I could feel the heat from those ovens—it was so real. And I had to keep running because if I stopped, the fire would get me. So, I would run and run until I would always just make it to where there was this split rail fence. But every time I started over the fence, the top rail would break away and I'd fall backwards. That was the place in the dream where I would always wake up.

I dreamed that dream for years, over and over. I never knew why. I was a real nosey kid when I was little. I must have overheard somebody talking about those ovens and what happened to my grandfather then started dreaming about it.

Finally, I told my mother about it.

"You can't possibly remember that place," she said. "I remember it. I remember it real well."

"Well, something gave me nightmares."

"No, you must have heard us talking about Pennsylvania. You were too young to remember anything."

The fiery coke ovens in Bunch's dream were haunting images in a reoccurring nightmare—a horrible memory of an episode in our family history. To heat a coke oven, a wood fire was first started that gradually increased in intensity. Coal was then added, and once the ovens were heated, they would burn continuously seven days a week until the fire brick in them burned out. In Westmoreland County, Pennsylvania, today, a person would have to travel the back roads of the old mining towns to find remnants of abandoned coke ovens that were built into the banks of hillsides.

Shortly after the death of his father and brother, my great-grandfather Luke became an ordained minister in the White Rock Baptist organization. Not long after that, he quit coal mining and began preaching in and around Westmoreland. Maybe carrying around the secret of his father's death created an inner desire for penitence and forgiveness.

Chapter Fourteen: Scientific Racism

In 2007, a man made the headlines when he shared the story of his father, who had revealed to him that they were Black, not White. The man said his father even went so far as to move the family to an inner-city neighborhood to be closer to "their kind of people," thinking this the right thing to do. The man's father believed he had been living a lie his whole life. He believed he was doing his son an injustice, keeping him from his *true* heritage. The man's story attracted attention from both Black and White America, especially Oprah Winfrey, and the media. Lifetime television even offered him a TV movie. On talk shows the man shared how, when he was a kid, he was attacked, tormented, and beaten up by the Black kids for being White and by the White kids for being Black *but* looking White.

After reading the story, I felt sorry for the man and his father. They were 21st century victims of centuries old White supremacist one-drop rule thinking. The man's father had believed the lie that "one drop of Black blood makes one Black," *a lie propagated by Walter Plecker and other White supremacists,* who were advocates of racial purity and eugenics, and believers in *scientific racism.*

Jacquelyn Moore, in her book, *Booker T. Washington, W.E.B. Du Bois, and the Struggle for Racial Uplift*, talked about the link between racism and Social Darwinism. Scientific racism made sense to most Whites, who already held prejudices and stereotypes of Blacks and who already believed themselves to be superior to Blacks. Jacquelyn shares the following theory as to why Social Darwinism caught on so rapidly in Western Europe and in the United States in the1800s:

> *Social Darwinism contributed heavily to the rise of racism in the Western world. Social scientists, trying to identify different subspecies within humanity, began to classify the world in terms of its different ethnic groups and to rank these groups in order of superiority. Naturally, they began with the assumption that western Europeans were the ideal, and so the more any ethnic group differed from that ideal, the more inferior that group must be. Most believed that intervening to help the weaker groups was simply delaying their inevitable end and interfering with the natural order. Others went as far as to advocate "eugenics," or selective breeding or desirable ethnic groups.*[25]

In America in 1924, Walter Plecker was waging his own war in America... a war against interracial marriage and multiracial people. As the Virginia State Registrar of Vital Statistics, Plecker "ordered application of the 1924 Virginia law in such a way that vital records were changed or destroyed" [26] and "...directed offices under his authority to change vital records and reclassify certain families as Black (or Colored) *without notifying them*. Many mulattoes, acting with pure intentions, came under fire from Plecker for registering as White even though that was how their parents had identified themselves. [27] Plecker delighted in telling these families that they were *not White*—only colored.

Virginia, as both a colony and a state, had led the way with laws prohibiting interracial relationships and marriage and Virginia's One-drop rule declared that anyone proven to have one drop of non-White blood was not legally White.[28] The binary world of the one-drop rule disregarded the self-identification both of people of mostly European ancestry who grew up in white communities, and of people who were of mixed race and identified as American Indian.[29]

The existence of mulattos *(*people with multiracial ancestry) greatly disturbed Plecker, who was convinced that mulatto offspring would slowly blend into the White race, and he referred to mulattos as rats that needed to be stopped. Plecker gave speeches to the American Public Health Association and Southern Medical Association, praising Virginia for taking the lead in preserving racial purity. Asserting that Virginia Indians were, in fact, "mixed-blooded negroes," Plecker also pressured state agencies into reclassifying Indians as "colored."[30]

Plecker's Racial Integrity Bill was introduced into the legislature in February 1924 and had the backing of the state's leading newspaper. But things immediately hit a snag when state senator *James S. Barron,* whose family had always proudly claimed to be descended from the union of John Rolfe and Pocahontas, realized that *the Bill would eliminate him from the White race*. He insisted that the Bill be amended so that "descendants of Pocahontas" could be classified as White. Therefore, a one-sixteenth or less of Indian blood ruling was granted for the descendants of Pocahontas and other Virginians to be considered White. Senator Barron then supported the Act on March 8, 1924, the same day *the Virginia Sterilization Law* was enacted.[31]

In 1930, *the United States Census Bureau, under pressure from White southern legislators,* stopped using the racial classification of mulatto altogether. *As a result, the long social recognition of mixed-race people was lost.*[32]

Fallout from the Census Bureau's reclassification of families who had lived their entire lives as White, in White communities, like their families before them, began to resonate across the states, many of which had passed their own one-drop laws and miscegenation laws forbidding interracial marriages. As a result, the restaurants, businesses, hotels, and schools that White and mulatto families had had once frequented or attended alongside other Whites suddenly became "off limits" to them.

Similar to the reaction to the petition prohibiting interracial marriages that had circulated in the 1800s, many White families with mulatto ancestry began to flee Pennsylvania in the 1930s. The segregation that came with the new racial reclassification made life unbearable for previously White families in southwestern Pennsylvania. So, families fled to other states, hoping the new laws would not follow them there, hoping for a new beginning.

Chapter Fifteen: Running from the Law

Plecker lobbied the US Census Bureau to drop the category of "mulatto" in the 1930 and later censuses. This deprived mixed-race people of recognition of their identity and contributed to a binary culture of hypodescent, in which mixed-race persons were often classified as the group with lower social status. Not until the 21st century did the census allow individuals to indicate more than one race or ethnic group in self-identification.[33]

—J. Douglas Smith

In 1930, life in Pennsylvania changed in a radical way for my great-grandfather, Luke Louis, and for the rest of my family as the familiar discrimination and segregation of "old Mississippi" reared its ugly head once again.

While his father, Blainey, had been Italian, great-grandpa Luke's mother, Josephine, was not—she was half-Cheyenne and half-Black Seminole. But it wasn't her Indian ancestry that caused trouble for her or her son's family. It was her *Negro* ancestry that caused the problem. Her Cheyenne ancestry meant nothing to the United States Census Bureau. It was the Black Seminole part that mattered...the fact that she had *Black* blood...Because *any degree of Black blood meant reclassification*. While her Seminole daughter-in-law, Willa-Nita, was allowed to retain her Indian classification, Josephine was not. According to the Aryan one-drop rule ideology, she was Negro *and only* Negro.

But the reclassification did not stop there.

The reclassification extended to Josephine's children and to their children's children. So great-Grandpa Luke and Great-Grandma Louisa, along with Grandpa Ed and Aunt Bunch, were also reclassified...*From White to Black* (Negro).

For over 100 years, Great-Grandma Louisa's family had lived in southwestern Pennsylvania as White. Her families Scotch, Dutch, Irish heritage had allowed for such a life—a life that was quickly stripped away in 1930. And she, along with her husband and children, was suddenly Black.

The following story is Aunt Bunch's story in her own words.

As far as my mother knew, she was White. Her mother was White. Her grandparents, Sylvester and Cornelia, and William O'Banion were White, and she had lived in a White neighborhood. My mother didn't know any other life. That's how they lived. And they had lived that way for a long, long time. Her father was Irish, so her maiden name was O'Banion. She was proud of that—very proud. When she got married, her father gave her a Tartan as a wedding gift—his Irish family tartan. All the Irish had tartans. Ours used to hang on our wall when we were kids. Before my mother died, she gave it to me. And I had it for a long time, but to this day, I don't know what happened to it.

Now my dad's father was Italian—pure Italian. His father wasn't mixed with nothing. My daddy had been born down in the south, in Mississippi [Vital Records record Alabama]. His last name was spelled L-O-U-I-S back then—that was the original spelling. The colored school changed it to L-E-W-I-S when we got older.

There was also Indian there on my dad's side. My grandmother, Josephine, she was Indian, half-Cheyenne and half-Seminole...Black Seminole...But she was fair, very fair. She had golden brown skin and real pretty long black hair that was mixed with gray. And she was tall and slender—not short like me. I remember her well. She was such a beauty. I loved my grandmother so much. That's also where the Negro came in, further up the line there on my grandmother's side.

Not long ago—in or about 2001, I visited Mt. Carmel Baptist Church in Winchester, Virginia. There was a guest speaker there that particular day—a senator from Washington, DC. As I sat there, I noticed that this man, this senator, kept staring at me. All through the service, he kept looking at me. It made me so nervous. Every time I looked up or happened to look in his direction, he'd be looking at me.

Well, of course, when everything was over, people were going up to him to talk to him and shake his hand, so I went up,

too. When it came my turn, before I could even get a word out, he grabbed hold of my hand and looked me straight in the eyes. Then he said with a real serious voice, "What tribe?"

I said, "I beg your pardon."

"What tribe are you from?"

"Well, we were always told it was Cheyenne."

"Oh. . . the rich tribe," he said, grinning real big.

"Well, that I don't know. They've never given me anything, and I never asked for anything." Then I asked him, "How in the world did you know to ask me that?"

To this day, I never forgot what he said to me. Leaning in, Bunch narrowed her eyes and spoke in a deep voice.

"One knows one's own."

I never forgot him. I remember he had an Indian name—it was Nighthorse.

The man who spoke at Aunt Bunch's church that day was Senator Ben Nighthorse Campbell, a Cheyenne Chief, who served Colorado as a United States Senator from 1992 to 2004. He is currently alive and well, living in

Colorado. Chief Nighthorse is a member of the Northern Cheyenne Tribe.

After the reclassification of Great-Grandpa Luke's family, he once again made plans to run away, this time taking his family with him. And after sending his mother ahead, he packed up his family and whatever would fit into the back of a friend's truck and left Westmoreland to join his mother and sister just across the state line in Clarksburg, West Virginia. His sister-in-law, Willa-Nita, left to return to her family in Oklahoma.

Although she was very young at the time, Aunt Bunch could recall her family making the move from Pennsylvania in 1931.

I **remember** being five or six years old when we moved to West Virginia from Pennsylvania. I don't remember how all of us kids got there. I don't know if it was by car, bus, or what, but when we got there, my grandmother Josephine was there, living with Aunt Georgey. When I saw my grandmother, I was so happy to see her. I ran and crawled up in her lap. I was just a little kid, but I can remember that clearly. That's not just something somebody told me. I remember because Aunt Georgey was such a mean woman. And she would not let me sit in my grandmother's lap. She wouldn't let me anywhere near her. She treated your grandfather the same way. Every time we tried to go near grandmother, Georgey would grab both of us and snatch us away. I cried so hard and carried on something terrible because I was so glad to see my grandmother again.

Georgia was her name. But everyone called her Georgey. She was older than my daddy and Gartha. My grandmother was married before she married my dad's father. Georgey was from that other marriage.

My parents left us with Aunt Georgey so they could go back to Pennsylvania to get some more of our things. We didn't own a car, so they hitchhiked the whole way there and back. I can remember my mother saying, "Ole Tom was right there walking beside us all the way back." She was talking about my cat, who I named Tom. We had to leave Tom in Pennsylvania, but my parents brought him back with them.

When my mother and father left us with Aunt Georgey, she was so nasty to us. Ohhhh. . .Let me tell you, she was the meanest, most hateful woman you'd ever want to meet. I truly, truly did not like that woman. And you know what? I never saw my grandmother again. We moved into our own place, and she died not too long after that. It makes me angry to this day just to think about it. William, my oldest brother, he hated her the most. He always used to say, "When that old woman dies, nobody's going to dig her grave but me!"

Well, she did die one day. It was a strange thing. She used to love to go to the riverbank to fish. Normally, she would take Frank with her because, for some reason, Frank was the only one of us Aunt Georgey liked. So, it was just plain luck one day that she didn't have Frank with her. But there she was on the riverbank when a sudden storm came up.

It started hailing real bad—big 'ole golf ball sized hail. And there wasn't any shelter for her to run and hide. So, the hail beat her in the head something terrible. She didn't die right away. It took about two or three months before she finally went on and died.

William said, "I am going to bury that woman and I am going to beat her in the face with my shovel as I'm burying her."

And he did bury her. The rest of us kids, we all snuck back there to the field to watch him bury her. And there he was out there shoveling dirt in on her just singing away. I can't remember what he was singing. It was probably something like, "I'm glad you're gone, you old rascal you."

Chapter Sixteen: Our Italian Neighborhood

People always thought I was Italian. I realize that most people now think of Italians as White. But back then, there were some White people who didn't like Italians. Italians got called names, too, just like Black people. They were discriminated against too back then. I guess everyone was in some way.

—Louise "Bunch" King

Standing on the stage in 2006 next to Grandpa Ed and Aunt Bunch, I shared with my newly acquainted family how Great-Grandpa Luke's father had been Italian and how our last name had originally been spelled *Louis*. I found out later that this news was a surprise revelation to just about everyone in the room.

While I can't remember all of the names and faces of the relatives I met that day, I do remember one young cousin in particular. She was nineteen years old and was the granddaughter of Aunt Bunch's brother, Frank, who had passed away in 1991. With a big grin on her face, she stopped me as I stepped off the stage.

Excitedly, she asked, "Do we really have Italian in our family?"

For a quick moment, I stared back at her, a little surprised by her question. The tone of her voice let me know she was serious and genuinely curious. Then I managed a quick head nod.

"Yes. Yes, we do," I finally managed to say.

She and I chatted for a brief moment then she was off to rejoin her Ohio family, who had driven in from Youngstown to celebrate with Aunt Bunch and Grandpa Ed.

Over the years, I have thought often about that moment and about my little cousin. Like Cornelia, she had light bright pale skin, brown eyes, and long pretty brown hair. I thought about how often I had looked at my family and our different shades and features—some White, some Black, some Indian—and wondered...why do we all look so different? Where did we come from? Now I wondered if my little cousin had been looking in the mirror all of her life asking the same questions.

Maybe the Italian revelation had answered some of her lifelong questions as well.

Growing up in Pennsylvania, Bunch and her brothers and sister had grown up in a culture of freedom, living as a White family until 1930 when the Census Bureau's racial reclassification law changed all of that. Overnight, the family went *from White to Black*. Leaving Pennsylvania and resettling in another state meant a new beginning for the Louis family. Getting back to *his* roots, Great-Grandpa Luke settled his family into an all-Italian neighborhood in Clarksburg, West Virginia. There they started life over, once more, as a White family (according to records).

A self-confessed eavesdropper, Aunt Bunch told about how she often hid under her parent's bed to listen in on the "grown up" conversations that took place between her parents and visiting neighbors. Listening to her funny and often touching stories about her brothers and sisters, friends and neighbors from her childhood made me wish even more that I had known her brothers and sisters, and her parents, especially

Great-Grandpa Luke. Some of her stories, however, were so revelatory, shocking, and heart-wrenching that I found myself very thankful I had never lived in such a day and time.

The following story is Aunt Bunch's story, in her own words.

When I was born, I was a little on the fat side. When my father saw me, he said, "She's just a little bunch." After having so many boys, my dad was happy to have another girl born into the family. I was named after my mother, Louisa, however, when I started school, they spelled my name with an E at the end-Louise, instead of with an A—Louisa—so all of my life I've been Louise.

I grew up in an Italian neighborhood in West Virginia. There were all Italians there in our neighborhood. And I loved it. We were in and out of each other's houses, especially me. I used to love to go visiting. That's how I learned to cook. I cooked at their houses. At Easter I would run around from house to house eating all the different foods. They would make those hot cross buns and those twists—twists were kind of like a donut—a raised donut, but they were twisted, and we would put powdered sugar on them. Nowadays, they have Italian festivals each year in Clarksburg, but back then, that was the closest thing we had to an Italian festival, running from house to house.

My mother was a good cook, too, but she cooked mostly southern food because that's what my dad liked to eat. I think we ate grits every day. Whatever my dad ate, we had to eat. That's why I went to eat at other houses a lot. My dad would eat Italian food, but he preferred more southern-style cooking.

There was a Black family that lived about a quarter of a mile away. Their name was Van Zandt. Their father was a minister, too. A little further lived a few more Black families, but that was about it. There weren't many Black families out our way and not any in our neighborhood, only Italians.

I was the eavesdropper in the family when I was a kid. I was small, so whenever I saw someone coming down the road toward the house, I would run and slide up under my parent's bed in the back bedroom. I knew that's where the grownups were going to go to talk. That's where they always went. The only way I learned anything at home was by crawling up under my parent's bed and listening in on their conversations. When I was little, kids did not get in no grown folks conversation.

"You can't sit here and listen to grown folks talk," my parents would say. Then they would send me out of the room. But I didn't like people keeping stuff from me. I was nosey. I just had to know what was going on, so I hid up under the bed and listened in.

My parent's room was the only private room we had. We had a family room, but nobody went in there except on holidays. The privacy was in the bedroom, so when I saw someone coming, I'd run and hide under the bed. I'd get there ahead of them, you see. They never knew I was there. I knew full well what would have happened to me if my parents would've caught me, but I did it anyway. I would hold my breath and lay real still. . . and just listen.

My dad was a great listener. He had a good sense of humor and could really make you laugh. So, people used to love to come over and sit on our porch and talk to my dad. But when they had something to say that they didn't want us kids to hear, they'd get up and head to the back of the house, to my parent's bedroom to talk in private. And every time they went to the back room, I was already there, hiding under the bed, listening.

Now there was a man who lived in our neighborhood. He was a White man. But he wasn't Italian. His last name was Elliot. I don't know why he lived there because, for some reason, people in our neighborhood were always giving him a hard time. All the kids used to talk about the man, saying he was an informant. I didn't know. But I knew there was something about him that made them not like him. One day, when I was hiding under the bed, I heard some of the men from our neighborhood talking about this man, Elliot.

They said, "He must be an informant. He's telling on us because things keep leaking out."

They didn't trust him you see because he wasn't Italian.

Then one day, here comes Mrs. Elliot down the road to visit my mother. My mother was a good listener, too, and she didn't fuss too much with people. She was a reverend's wife, so ladies used to like to come talk to her. I was sitting on the porch being nosey when I saw Mrs. Elliot coming up the hill, so off I ran to the bedroom to hide. I slid up under the bed and waited. Soon enough, here they came, she and my mother.

"I don't know why they keep bothering him. Somebody is telling secrets on them, and they think it's him. But it's not him," she said, crying to my mother.

Now I didn't know whether he was doing it or not. I was only about nine or ten years old at the time. I was just the eavesdropper you see. I was just there to get the gossip!

There was another man in our neighborhood. His Italian name was Biago, but my father just called him, "Bill." His last name was Defazio. I think his English last name was Davis. Our name was Louis, but then it got changed to Lewis when we had to change schools. I think the same thing must have happened with his name, Defazio. But this Bill Defazio and my dad could pass for brothers. They went anywhere and everywhere together around Clarksburg. They were inseparable, so people just assumed they were brothers. He and my dad were the closest of friends. Besides us, my dad didn't have any other family in West Virginia. His dad had died, then his brother Gartha, then his mother, and his sister Georgey died after that. So, we were all my dad had left. I think that's why my father was so close to Bill Defazio. Bill reminded my dad of Gartha. My dad was very close to

Gartha.

Now Bill had a son named Joe—Joe Defazio. One day Joe came over to the house to talk to my dad. After talking for a minute or so, they got up and headed to the back room. Of course, I was already there waiting under the bed ready to listen in.

People who knew my dad always called him Rev (short for Reverend) because he was a minister.

"Rev. Louis, there's going to be trouble tonight," Joe told my dad. "You need to keep your kids in the house tonight."

"I understand. Thank you, Joe," my dad said. "I appreciate you telling me."

My dad didn't ask any questions. He wasn't a nosey person like me.

Our house sat at the top of the hill overlooking our neighborhood. That night, Martha and I were sitting out on the porch. It was real quiet outside. Then Martha got up, walked to the edge of the porch, stretched out her arms real wide, and sighed really loud. "Oh, I wish something would happen around here. It's sooooo boring."

Now why did she say that? She just wished up trouble. Suddenly, all hell broke loose... And we heard all this commotion further down the hill, people yelling and fighting and carrying on. Mom and Dad came running out of the house and drug us back into the house. Then they hurried

and shut the door and closed the blinds so we couldn't look outside to see what was happening. After a while, the uproar died down and it got quiet again.

I never found out what happened that night. And I didn't ask. You had to know when to not ask too many questions in our neighborhood and when to just go about your own business.

Sometimes at night, when it got dark, we would see crosses burning out in the fields off in the distance. The KKK (Ku Klux Klan) was around back then.**

I don't remember anyone talking about them much at that time, but they were around, and everybody knew it. Sometimes they would burn crosses out in the fields to try and scare people. But the KKK never came in our neighborhood. I can tell you that for sure.

They knew better.

There was a group in our neighborhood called the

** The Ku Klux Klan is a secret organization founded in 1915. But it was active for several years after the Civil War in the southern United States. It aimed to suppress the newly acquired powers of blacks. But it was directed against blacks, Catholics, Jews and foreign born (*Dictionary.com Unabridged*. Retrieved December 04, 2015, from http://dictionary.reference.com/browse/ku-klux-klan).

Blackhand.[***] People paid them for protection. They were Italian, too, all of them, but they were corrupt. They had a lot of money, at least what we considered money back then—more money than most people in our neighborhood. Some people called them Mafia, but not to their face. They lived there along with us and everyone else.

Our neighborhood was called Union Heights. And it had such a bad reputation in town and around Clarksburg. All you had to do was mentioned to people in town that you lived in Union Heights and people would gasp in shock.

"Ohhhh. . . You live in that place?"

It got so bad that my dad got a petition

[***] The roots of the Black Hand can be traced to the Kingdom of Naples as early as the 1750s. However, the term that is normally used in English specifically refers to the organization established by Italian immigrants in the United States during the 1880s who, though fluent in their Southern Italian regional dialects, had no access to Standard Italian or even a grammar school education. A minority of the immigrants formed criminal syndicates, living alongside each other. By 1900, Black Hand operations were firmly established in the Italian-American communities of major cities including New York, Philadelphia, Chicago, New Orleans, Scranton, San Francisco, Olean, NY and Detroit. In 1907, a Black Hand headquarters was discovered in Hillsville, Pennsylvania, a village located a few miles west of New Castle, Pennsylvania. * Retrieved 20:30, October 14, 2015 from https://en.m.wikipedia.org/wiki/Black_Hand_(extortion). Above picture from Library of Congress of Blackhand members arrested in Harrison County, West Virginia in the 1930s.

together to get the name changed. He took it to the courthouse in town and it passed. Everyone agreed to change the name to Parkview because, next to where we lived, there was a park, which sat on a hill. Our house sat at the top of that hill. Down the hill about a mile was a hard, paved road called Anmoore Road—this road ran all the way through into town.

Across from our house, at the top of the hill was a little bridge. People from other neighborhoods used to use this bridge as a short cut to cross over to the other side of the park. Well. . . There was this boy who lived in another neighborhood. His name was Billy. He wasn't Italian. But for some reason, whenever this boy saw me or Ed, he would start calling us names—bad names. And you know what names I'm talking about. The bad names they used to call Italians back then.

I could not stand that boy. And what made me so mad was, he didn't even know us. He didn't even know our names. But you can bet I knew his. I had made it my business to find it out.

One afternoon, Ed and I were sitting out on the front porch, minding our own business. All of a sudden, we heard whistling. Then this boy Billy came bopping along across the hill toward the bridge. Do you know, as soon as he saw us, he stopped and started in on us. Then he grinned real big and went along across the bridge. Well, I sat there, mad as usual, watching him walk away. Just then Momma and Daddy came out of the house. Daddy patted us on the head and said, "We are going down to the church for a minute. You two sit here on the porch. We'll be right back."

We watched them walk off down the road. Once they were out of sight, I jumped off the porch and turned to Ed.

"I am tired of that boy calling us names. I'm not gonna take it anymore! I'm gonna go teach him a lesson."

"Count me in!" Ed shouted as he jumped off the porch.

We ran across the hill there to the little bridge. And I crawled underneath it on one side while Ed ran across and crawled underneath on the other side. Then we waited.

Sure enough, here came Billy. We could hear him whistling away. He liked to whistle. But I waited until I heard his feet hit the bridge then I crawled out and jumped up on the bridge. Ed crawled out from the other end and jumped up on the bridge. We had him blocked in. You should have seen the look on his face. He didn't know what to think.

I said, "I am tired of you calling us names," then Ed and I jumped him.

Now let me say this: I had been in some fights as a kid, but that was a hard one. Ed and I wrestled with that boy and oh, let me tell you, I was ever so glad Ed was there to back me up. I don't think I could have beaten him on my own. But the two of us together got it done.

After the fight, Billy ran off, and Ed and I ran back home

and jumped back up on the porch. We sat there, pretending like nothing happened. Here come Momma and Daddy back up the street. Daddy walked up on the porch and patted us on our heads again. He smiled at us, probably thinking, "Oh, aren't they just so cute." Ed and I just sat there, looking all innocent and grinning real big, like a couple little angels.

Billy didn't do any more name-calling after that. We saw him around and he still crossed the bridge, but whenever he did. . . He kept his mouth shut.

I stopped hiding under the bed for a while after I heard more than I wanted to hear one day. I saw my mom coming down the street with this lady, so I went and hid under the bed. I regretted hiding under the bed that day. What I heard gave me nightmares.

My mother was a midwife, you see, and she and this woman got to talking in the room about this woman in our neighborhood who was pregnant and how the baby died inside the mother. My mother was telling this other woman about how the baby had come out mortified. Now I didn't know what that mortified meant, but I looked it up in the dictionary later on. So, there I was hiding under the bed listening to my mother talking about how the baby died, how it was rotten inside of the mother, and how the mother was passing the baby one piece at a time . . . one arm . . . one leg... And how the mother died, too, from all that poison inside her. You talk about scared. Honey, I wanted to come out from under that bed so fast. My body was shaking, and my knees were knocking so hard, I thought they might hear it. But I knew better than to come out. I would have been in a worse fix if my mother saw me.

After they left, I snuck out of the room and went to look up that word—mortified. I didn't even know how to spell it, but I found it—it meant "decayed, rotten."

Well, my hiding-under-the-bed days stopped for a long time after hearing that story. But that was how we found things out back then. The grownups didn't like to talk around us kids. Anything we found out came from me hiding under the bed. My brothers and sister knew I hid under the bed. Whenever we saw someone coming to the house to talk to our parents, they'd whisper to me, "Go, Bunch, go."

After the person left, I'd run back to my brothers and sister and give them the scoop. They never told on me.

My father had only gone as far as second grade in school. He never learned to read or write, except for his name, which he had taught himself to write. But my dad was smart, real smart. When he became a minister, he began to teach himself how to read and write using the Bible.

My dad built a lot of churches around the city—even one as far away as Charleston. When I was a teenager, he would say to me, "Bunch, draw me a church," and I would draw different pictures of churches then I'd take 'em to my dad. He'd tell me to add this or add that. And I would. Do you know my dad would go build a church that looked almost exactly like my picture? He would figure in the feet, the cost of the materials, and everything. I think one of those churches is still standing today, out there on Anmoore Road.

Chapter Seventeen: From White to Black

Stripping families of all other ancestry and racial heritage, the One-Drop Law reclassified as Negro or colored anyone with even a very small portion of Black ancestry.[34]
—Pauli Murray

In the 1930s and 1940s, laws relying heavily on Aryan one-drop rule thinking reclassified thousands of mulatto families as Negro, or colored, because they had or were *believed to have* at least *one drop* of Black blood in their ancestry. Although many groups challenged this action, most were overruled by the United States Supreme Court, who upheld each state's segregation and miscegenation laws.

In the 1940s and 1950s, Clarksburg, West Virginia, had color lines of its own to enforce segregation—from the local Robinson Grand movie theatre and its designated "colored-only" section in the upper balcony, to the "colored-only" restrooms and restaurants around town.

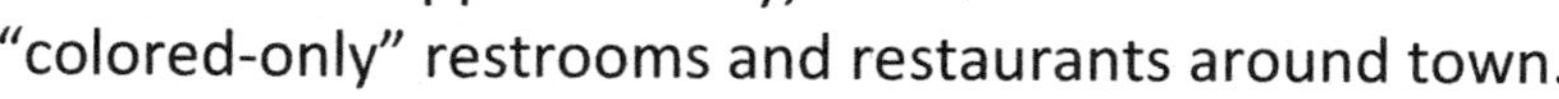

Up until she was eleven years old, Bunch and her brothers and sister had attended school in their neighborhood in a one-room *Little House on the Prairie* style schoolhouse. Then their world went from White to Black overnight as the one-drop rule once again reared its ugly head and subsequently reclassified the family as Negro, subjecting them to the strict laws of segregation. Laws which meant they could no longer attend their all-White school. Instead, they had to, by law, attend the only school in town for Negro children, Kelly Miller Negro School. Life for Aunt Bunch, Grandpa Ed, and the rest of the Louis family changed once more—*forever.*

For the first ten years of her life, Bunch had experienced all of the

privileges of White America. Now she and her brothers and sisters had to quickly learn to live under the weight of the bigotry and discrimination they began to encounter for the first time in their lives, from both sides of the color line. However, the biggest challenge was learning to think of themselves as Negro *and only Negro* as society began to respond to them as Black and not as White. Unfortunately, learning to live their lives as *colored* children would not be the only change in their lives.

The name Louis had been my great-grandfather's last name—his father's Italian family name since his father had immigrated to America in the 1800s. However, in 1939, with one stroke of a pen, the Louis family name was carelessly wiped away as officials at Kelly Miller Negro School recorded the names of the Louis children, using the more traditional English spelling of Lewis.

Originally named Water Street Colored School in 1919, the school name was changed in 1920 in honor of Kelly Miller, a Black scientist, mathematician, author, and influential figure among Black Americas at the time. It was the only school for Negro, or colored, children in Clarksburg. Since the "colored" population of Clarksburg was not large enough to justify more than one school, Kelly Miller served several counties. Negro and colored students from other counties were bused into Clarksburg on Monday mornings, boarded at their counties expense during the week, then returned by bus to their homes on Friday evening. During Aunt Bunch's school days, the school served grades first through twelfth.

The following story is Aunt Bunch's story in her own words.

I stayed in the first grade for two or three years at our little shotgun school. Not because I wasn't smart, but because I just wouldn't go to school. Our little one-room schoolhouse had six grades in it—just like Little House on the Prairie. You had about four or five students in first and second grade at that school. As the grades got higher, the numbers got smaller. The same teacher taught all six grades. That's why I skipped school a lot. I was bored. You see, while she was teaching those other grades, I was taking it all in, too. I wasn't playing around or cutting up because I was dumb, I just thought I already knew it all. And back up behind the school out where we lived there was a hickory nut tree and a walnut tree. And I liked to climb the nut trees—probably because I was a nut.

Finally, they made me go to school when they started busing the colored students into Kelly Miller. My parents didn't make a big deal about us having to go to Kelly Miller. And we didn't talk about it.

They told us, "You have to go to the colored school."

That was all they said. They didn't say why. They didn't have to. I wanted to go to school with my friends in our neighborhood, but I couldn't. And that was that. I wasn't happy with having to go to school, any school. I wanted to just run and play and climb trees.

The most difficult thing about that experience was, we had never thought of ourselves as colored, or as Black. We knew, back on my dad's mother's side, that there was some Black—but I don't remember anyone ever making a big deal about it up until then.

The Black students at Kelly Miller tried their best to bully me. But I gave it right back to them. It was because of my looks you know . . . because of my skin color and my long hair. Let me tell you, I was a flip something in school. I had no shape at all, just straight up and down. And I had this long hair—hair so long I could sit on it. It wasn't unheard of for me to toss my head back and stick my nose in the air when somebody made me mad. So, I was a loner in school. I never liked being around a whole lot of people. When I got to Kelly Miller, I couldn't just up and leave anymore to go climb trees. I had to stay in school. And I hated that.

It didn't take much to make me mad. I had a temper. And it got me in a lot of fights at Kelly Miller, especially with boys. The boys used to call me, "Miss Untouchable." I found this out years later when I ran into a man who had gone to Kelly Miller with me. He told me the boys used to call me "Miss Untouchable" because of the way I acted.

He said, "You would walk into the room like an inspector, like you worked there, with your head stuck up in the air."

Once, when I was visiting a church in Martinsburg, I ran into a woman who knew me from Kelly Miller. She told me the same thing.

She said, "I didn't think I would like you when you first came to church here. As soon as you walked in the church, I recognized you right away. I remembered you from Kelly Miller. I thought, "Oh, no! There she is." You used to walk around school like you owned it, like you were so much better than everyone."

Well, I never thought I was better than anyone. It wasn't that at all. And I wasn't stuck up like they thought. I was just very sure of myself—and I'll never apologize for that. That's just the way I was raised, confident. I was very proud of who I was. I wasn't raised to be scared of nobody. And I wasn't afraid to let people know it.

When I went to Kelly Miller, Mrs. Green was my first-grade teacher, Helen Thomas was my second-grade teacher, and Mrs. Moss was my third-grade teacher. It wasn't long before I caught up with my brothers, Ed, Frank, and Rob. They were older than me, but we all ended up in the same grade—all four of us. Then I left them all back there in the third grade.

My fourth-grade teacher was Mrs. Johnson—what a mean old woman she was. Truth told— I don't think the woman ever had a husband. We called her, "Old Maid."

Now let's see. . . I don't remember my fifth-grade teacher, but my sixth-grade teacher was Mrs. Reddix. I remember because my sixth-grade class was so big they had to split the class up. Mr. Billy Williams took over the other sixth grade class. They took us girls and put us over there with him, but that man had no control over us—none whatsoever. I had to sit in Mr. Williams's class all year. And the only thing I learned that year was how to make spit balls. I shot the principal, Mr. Saunders with a spit ball one day. I thought he was one of the boys coming in the door, so I let loose with a spit ball. "Who did that?" he shouted. But I just sat there looking way off out the window like I didn't even know he was there.

But nobody told on me. They knew better.

By seventh grade, I was studying in the high school books. I had Mr. Franklin as my homeroom teacher. That seventh-grade class so big—there were about 70-79 kids in one class until they split us into two classes. My sister Martha was in high school. I realized they were teaching me out of the same book she had in high school. So Martha and I just shared books.

In the eighth grade I had Mr. Franklin again. He taught Negro History—and you had better learn it. He was also my literature teacher. He lived right there on Ben Street, right behind the school.

It seemed like I was always doing something for him to get on me about. That man gave me the blues...I had detention all the time.

One day in class, he said, "I want you to learn the poem, 'If', and I want you to do it in one hour." Well, I looked at him and rolled my eyes. And that made him mad. So he said, with an attitude, "And since you rolled your eyes at me, I want you to learn 'Flanders Field' also!"

At the end of the day, after he had dismissed the whole class, he called me up to his desk. "If you recite both the poems I assigned you, then you can go."

I can still remember that poem. I had a strong memory. So, I learned that poem and "Flanders Field" in one hour—and I didn't leave an 'a' or 'b' out. I recited both those poems perfectly, word for word.

[Here, Bunch recites the poems, "If" and "Flanders Field," word for word.]

Then I flipped my long braids back over my shoulders and walked right out of the room. When he met my mother, he told her, "That child. . . She's a fresh something."

Most of the kids in the neighborhood I had grown up with still treated us the same—that didn't change. But there were other people, other kids who knew we went to Kelly Miller. Those kids treated us like we were colored. You know. . . I didn't think about it much then, but I did when I got older.

That was the first time I heard the word nigger. I was eleven years old. I had never heard that word before. I had never heard it when we lived in the Italian neighborhood. But one day, when I was walking home from school, this girl—she was a White girl—she yelled that word out at me. I didn't know she was talking to me at first. It almost passed me by. But then I realized she was talking to me. She made me so mad, I took off running after her—I chased her all the way home. She tried to run into her house— I guess she thought she would be safe inside. But that didn't stop me. I ran into the house after her and caught her by the hair. Then her mother grabbed hold of me and drug me outside.

I waited for her to come back outside, but she never did—and it's a good thing. I went home and told my mother what happened.

"Bunch, you can't go running up into a person's house

like that. That's just not proper." That's all she had to say about it. It makes me laugh now when I think about it.

That girl and I became friends not long after that. Her name was Margaret, and sometime later, I asked her why she called me that name. She said she didn't know what she was saying—she just said it.

I told her, "You better be careful about what you say. I could have really hurt you."

And I would have, too.

But we became friends. We were in the same grade. We used to talk about how nice it would be if we could go to the same school. But that didn't happen. I had to go to Kelly Miller. And Margaret got to ride the bus. All the White kids got to ride the bus.

I was also mistaken for being Syrian once. There was a Syrian family that lived down the road from our house. And I was walking just a little way from their house when the mother came out yelling.

"Sarah... Come home now!"

She was looking straight at me, but I just looked right back at her. I didn't think anything about it.

Then she yelled again, "Come here Sarah, now."

I looked around and I didn't see anybody else, so I yelled back to her.

"I'm not Sarah!"

Now I knew Sarah. We had played together a few times,

but I wasn't her.

By that time, the real Sarah pops out from around the house. Her mom stood there looking at us—from me to Sarah, and from Sarah to me, like, "Which one is Sarah?" It was a funny thing. We did look just a like, she and I—same skin color, same hair.

All the teachers at Kelly Miller were Black. All the staff was Black, too. It was truly an all-Black school—no White students and no White teachers at all.

To get to Kelly Miller, we had to ride the streetcar into town. I think about how my brothers and sisters, and I had to walk all the way down the hill from where we lived in Park View (which is called Anmoore now), then all the way down Anmoore Road, which was a long road. Then we had to walk up this long hill to catch the streetcar into town to get to Kelly Miller School. To this day, it makes me angry when I think about the school buses that passed us on the road. They were going the same direction that we were going—to town—into Clarksburg. But we weren't allowed to ride the bus because we were Black.

I always took a short cut to and from school. I would cut through this pasture and crawl under the fence that surrounded it. And every day I would go home so dirty because there was this old bull that was always after me in that pasture. But I would tease him something terrible. Then I'd run from him, crawl up under the fence real fast, and stick my tongue out at him. Back then, I wasn't afraid of nothing.

The streetcar went all the way down Main Street out to where all the rich folks lived in Golf Plaza. Out in Golf Plaza, the streetcar tracks ran up Pike Street and came down Main Street. After we caught the streetcar into town, we'd get off on Pike Street. Then we'd cut through the alley there to walk down Water Street to Kelly Miller.

After Brown v. Board of Education in Topeka, Kansas (1954) challenged segregated school systems as being inherently unequal, the United States Supreme Court ordered the integration of all public schools. Kelly Miller School continued to operate until 1956. E. B. Saunders proudly served as the principal of Kelly Miller from 1919 to 1956 when the school closed. The portion of Water Street where the school is located from Washington Ave to the dead end was renamed E. B. Saunders Way some time in the 1990s in honor of the former beloved Principal.

In the spring of 1990, the Kelly Miller Alumni Association laid the groundwork for what was to become known as The West Virginia Black Heritage Festival, Inc. The first Black Heritage Festival began on September 22, 1990, and was held on E. B. Saunders Way in front of Kelly Miller School. Graduates of Kelly Miller and their families came from all over the United

States to attend the festival, including Aunt Bunch and Grandpa Ed. Sitting in lawn chairs in front of Kelly Miller School, they recalled the times they had walked down that same street after riding the streetcar into town and down Pike Street.

(Below: Grandpa Ed attending the Kelly Miller Reunion in 2012)

(Aunt Bunch and her brother, Grandpa Ed, at Kelly Miller

Chapter Eighteen: The Walton's of West Virginia

It's never too late to become what we might have been.
—George Eliot

My great-grandpa Luke tried so hard to make life different for his children. He wanted them to be free from the yokes of discrimination and segregation and to never know the limitations, poverty, and sense of inferiority that came from living on the Black side of the color line.

I have often thought of Aunt Bunch, Grandpa Ed, and the rest of their brothers and sisters and wondered how different their lives would have been had they not been subjected to one-drop rule thinking, reclassification, and segregation. How different would their lives have been had they been left alone and allowed to continue living their lives in their Italian neighborhood, pursuing their dreams without the imposed boundaries of segregation?

Reclassification and relegation to the Negro side of the color line meant the Louis family had to learn a whole new way of life. No longer classified as White, they had to learn to live according to the rules and boundaries society had set for Negroes—rules that required them to attend Negro schools, to marry Negro husbands and Negro wives, and to work the jobs (many of the menial) that society determined were proper for

Negroes to work.

"**Do** you remember the TV Show, *The Walton's*?" Aunt Bunch asked as the two of us sat on her front porch, taking in the night air. "I was sitting at home one night watching *The Walton's* and I thought, 'Now wait a minute—same number of children, same order. We match perfectly—four boys and three girls.' John Boy was my oldest brother William, Mary Ellen was my oldest sister Martha, Jason was my brother Frank, Ben was my brother Robert, Erin was me (Louise), Jim Bob was my little brother Ed, and Elizabeth was our younger sister Sarah, who passed away.' I think that's why I always loved that show. It always reminded me of my family."

The following is Aunt Bunch's story in her own words.

I met my husband, Emmett Wilkinson, at Kelly Miller. I remember he was five years ahead of me. My sister Martha plotted to introduce me to him. She was engaged to a boy named Amos Perry, who she had met at Kelly Miller. Martha asked me to go with her one day to Amos's house. She kept insisting I go with her, so I did. When we got to the house, there was Emmett sitting up in Amos's house grinning at me real big. I realized I had been set up.

Emmet and I liked each other right off. And after I graduated high school, we got married. We moved into a little place right there across the street from

Kelly Miller on Water Street. Then Emmett joined the Army, so he was gone quite a bit. Your granddaddy also joined the Army around that time, so your grandmother, Deanny, she came to live with me.

Several of the women on the street, including me, would sit and talk in the evenings on the porch of a woman named Virginia Taylor. Virginia lived right there next to Mt. Zion Baptist Church, across the street from Kelly Miller. Virginia was the woman who taught me how to be a lady. She taught a lot of us how to be ladies.

Virginia would say, "Always be a lady. Always speak like a lady and act like a lady. Always dress like a lady. Let the men guess what's underneath. Hold your head up high when you walk. You might be poor, but you don't have to act like you're poor."

Now Virginia's husband. . . He was the most handsome man you ever wanted to see. And all the ladies would just go limp and swoon whenever he walked by. But the funniest thing was . . . well. . . Virginia was no beauty. We all used to wonder and whisper. . . 'Howwww did she get that beautiful man?' We figured it out real fast. She got him . . . by being a lady.

Virginia used to teach all of us, but I listened to every word she said and took it to heart. When I got older, I became the personnel manager for Kmart. I taught the female employees professional etiquette —how to walk and how to dress. I got so tired of seeing girls walking around the store looking so sloppy, not knowing how to dress, with their bra straps riding up their backs stuck up around their necks. And I wasn't the only one who noticed. The store manager had noticed, too.

He asked me one day, "Louise, can't you help these women? You always look so professional and so nice."

"Well, I can try."

Virginia had taught me, so I figured I would pass on what I learned from her. She was truly a wonderful woman.

You only had one chance with my father. He would tell you one time—then you didn't get any more chances. My oldest brother William [Bloomy Louis] learned this the hard way. He did something one day, and my daddy told him not to do it again. Well, William must have thought my dad was just talking, so he did it again anyway. My daddy didn't say a thing, not a word. He just reached over and picked up one of those brick liners. Brick liners look a lot like nine tails with metal on the end. Now at first, Daddy was only going to warn William, but when William saw Daddy pick up that brick liner, he took off running. That was his second big mistake. When he took off running from my dad, my dad took off after him. He ran and ran with Daddy right behind him. They ended up down by the railroad tracks and William tripped and fell and that was all she wrote. My daddy swatted him with that brick liner, steadily telling him... "get up." The rest of us kids, we just watched from a far, in the distance. At home, later that evening, when it was just us kids, we tried to get William to talk about it.

"Don't ever run from Dad," was all he said. And we believed him.

William was a quiet boy. He was tall and he was handsome, but he never said much to anyone. He tried to keep to himself, but he was somehow always ending up in a fight. He got in a lot of fights. Boys would pick at him because he was quiet. They thought he was weak, but he wasn't.

There was one Black family that we knew of named Van Zandt, who lived about a mile or so down the road from us. William went to Kelly Miller with their daughter Mary. William and Mary eventually fell in love, married, and had seven children: Joseph, Maurice, William Jr., Tommy, Mary, George, and Nash.

On August 19th, 1967, on my daughter Serena's 21st birthday, I was at home, sick in bed with the flu. I got a phone call from the police. They told me William had been killed in a car accident. I remember that day so clear. I was so sick that when I heard the news, my first thought was, "Oh, poor Momma must be devastated." I started to call her when I remembered she had died two years earlier. I was so sick, I had forgotten. But Momma was the first one I thought of when I heard about William.

William and the family had all gone fishing and were driving home on one of those narrow back roads when a coal truck came around the corner and hit their car—head on. They never saw it coming. Big Mary, it killed her instantly, and my brother William, he died right away, too. Little Nash, little Mary, and Tommy were all in the car with William and Big Mary. Tommy didn't die right away, he died later. Little Mary had a broken leg and a concussion. And little Nash suffered a concussion, a broken arm, and a broken leg.

I didn't think I would make it to the funeral. The doctor had told me not to go anywhere. That was hard because someone had to make funeral arrangements. You see, William and I were always the ones who made all the arrangements in the family. William and I were the ones who planned my dad's funeral. I was there with my mother when my dad died. Now I had to bury my big brother. He was also the one that I always leaned on in hard times. Now he was gone. But I was too sick to make any arrangements. So the family made the funeral arrangements. But I got well enough to make it to the funeral.

If you don't think anything good could ever come out of a horrible situation like that, believe me, I know it can. William's son, little Nash, was in a bad state of retardation before the car accident. Back then, nobody really knew what to call it—maybe some kind of cerebral palsy. With Nash, wherever they put him, that's where he stayed—if they laid him down, that's where he stayed—if they sat him on the floor, that's where he stayed. The doctors said he would never walk, he would never talk, he would never go to school, nothing, and before he was nine years old, he would probably die. This child could do absolutely nothing, but he was the cutest little boy. I adored him.

The amazing thing was... something in that accident unscrambled that child's brain. Do you know, when Nash came out of that hospital in Morgantown, something was right with that child. He still had the retardation, but not to the point where he couldn't learn. He also began to walk, and he began to talk. Eventually, he started going to school. He joined the Special Olympics team. There were so many things that child began to do after the accident.

Each summer he would come to Virginia to stay with me. I would keep him for about two weeks. He loved it here. When the time would come for him to go home, he never wanted to leave. Clare, his aunt, had always wanted him. Her husband's name was Nash and little Nash had been named after him. Clare had never had any children of her own, so she kept Mary and Nash and raised them. Do you know that child is still living today? He lives in Texas with his brothers, Joe and William, and his sister Mary.

Martha, my older sister, was nosey. When she didn't have her nose stuck in a book, she was always talking to people and asking questions, trying to get information out of people. She would have made a great private investigator or a reporter of some kind. She was always interrogating us, especially my dad, asking him questions. She was always trying to get information out of my dad about his past. Martha could really wear you down. And she would just wear on dad with her questions until he'd finally start talking just to get her to leave him alone.

One day, Martha managed to get it out of my dad that we had a half-sister. Well, why'd he tell her that? She really went to work on him then. She got my dad to give her names and places where this sister was supposed to live. Martha was determined to find this girl. Her name was Estella, and she was from my dad's previous marriage, or relationship. Martha started writing letters to all different places in the south, trying to track down Estella. She'd go to the library to make phone calls because we didn't have a phone.

Then in came a letter one day from somewhere down south. It was from Estella. She had gotten one of Martha's letters and wrote her back. She said she wanted to come and live with us. I remember my dad getting us all together in the kitchen and asking us what we thought about her coming. She was our sister and we all wanted her to come, so my dad sent her the money to come to West Virginia.

When we started going to Kelly Miller School, Martha met a boy by the name of Amos Perry. The two were married right after Martha graduated from high school. It didn't take long before they started having kids. And the kids just kept on coming, one right after another; she had a baker's dozen of them. Unfortunately, not all of them lived. Martha loved kids and was very good at raising kids. My sister was a great mother. But she never stopped her exploring. She would take her kids up to caverns to go cave exploring. Martha always wanted to travel. She just never got a chance to. That's why she used to love to read those books about faraway places. She was curious about the world.

Martha knew so much about our family history—more than anyone else. My sister was the smartest person I knew. As her kids got older, Martha took a job as a janitor. And she worked as a janitor all of her life. She retired from that job and was very proud of that.

Estella was our half-sister. She had come to live with us with her baby, James—James Brown. Her last name was Brown too. She had been married, but she didn't say much about the baby's father, and my daddy didn't ask her about him. She stayed with us for about three years until my father put her out. You see, Estella hadn't sowed all her wild oats. She was always wearing those shiny dresses and fishnet stockings. And she would stay out all hours of the night. Then she'd try to sneak back in the house. One night my dad caught her sneaking in and told her he wasn't going to have it—she had to go. Estella said she would leave but she was "taking James with her." When she said that, my dad was fit to be tied.

He said, "You are not taking that child out of this house. If I have to stand on a chair to knock you down, I will."

My dad said this you see because Estella was tall—real tall—taller than my daddy. And he didn't want her taking James just anywhere. He was just a little boy. My dad wanted her to settle down first. In the end, my dad won and Estella moved out. She left James with us. And my mother and my father raised James along with us until Estella eventually settled down and came to get him.

After my dad died, Estella left West Virginia and moved to Detroit. I think I only saw Estella one more time after that before she died. We both used to joke and say we were going to live to be one hundred. She was ninety-six years old when she died. She almost made it.

Robert was my second oldest brother. He was tall and big-boned, with red skin. And he was the healthiest person you ever saw. He had never been sick a day in his life. Then one day, he got into a hornets' nest. He had been messing around with the nest—hitting at it with a stick. Next thing he knew, those hornets came swarming out of the nest and chased him. If there wasn't any water to jump in, they would get you. Well, Robert didn't have any water to jump in, so they got him. He came home swollen up with big welts all over him. My mother bathed him in milk. Then she put some of her home-made medicine on him. And she put one of my dressing gowns on him. He had to walk around in that gown for days until he got better. Boy, did we laugh at him.

My parents never took us to the doctor. We couldn't afford it. My mom used to go out in the woods. And she would come back with all kinds of plants and stuff. She also grew her own herbs. That's what she would use on us. She'd mix up all kinds of concoctions and make ointments. And they all worked.

Robert was the one who used to take me hunting, he and Ed. I was such a little tomboy, probably because I used to run around behind my brothers all the time, trying to do whatever they did. All my brothers liked to hunt. One night we went hunting for coon [raccoon]. We didn't eat them, but there were some families who lived up in the hills who liked to eat it. And they'd pay my brothers money for the meat.

Anyway, when you're hunting coon, you have to go at night because that's when they come out. Then you chase it up a tree and shine the light on it. And the light makes it freeze. Then you shoot it in the tree. Well, one night Robert and I. . . I think Frank was there, too. . . But we chased this coon into a tree. Then we shined the light and like always, it froze.

"Okay, Bunch, shoot it!" Robert yelled.

I lifted my gun and took aim, but I couldn't pull the trigger.

"Go ahead, shoot, shoot!" He and Frank both started shouting.

But I just couldn't do it. It looked so scared. I just couldn't shoot the poor thing.

I cried out, "No-o-o! I can't shoot it. I can't do it."

So Robert gave up.

"Oh alright, let's go home Frank. She can't go hunting with us anymore. She's turning into a girl."

Robert married a girl named Virginia Harris. Virginia was from Ohio. She and Robert had five children: Elaine, Sissy, Garry, Jenny, and Lukey, who was named after my dad.

One day, it was a crazy thing, Robert was out chopping wood for the winter then he went over to his daughter's house and chopped some wood for her. He got it all stacked up and was getting ready to go somewhere else to chop some more wood.

Suddenly, he said, "Uh-oh. . . Uh oh, Gin—this is it."

He had a sudden heart attack right there on the spot. He was rushed to the hospital, but he died before he got there. Robert had never been sick a day in his life.

My older brother Frank was so handsome. My, oh my, he was such a ladies man. Women would just fall all over my brother Frank. They just loved him...And Frank loved women. I used to just sit back and watch girls make a fool of themselves over my brother. It was fun to watch.

Frank's other love was boxing. He loved to box. Any chance he got, he would put on those gloves and find someone to box with. He used to grab me, hold me down, and tie those boxing gloves on my hands. He would tie them so tight I could not get them off. Then he would start hitting me. And he would keep hitting me until I hit him back.

"Come on. . . Fight back. . . Fight. . . Fight!" He would shout at me.

Well, I didn't want to fight him, so I would never hit him back until one day when he hit me kinda hard. And it made me mad. That's when I started fighting back. I got him real good one time, real hard right in the nose. I hit him so hard his nose started bleeding. After that, he stopped and took off his gloves. I was ready to hit him again. But I didn't.

He said, "Here, let me take your gloves off. I know you can take care of yourself now. I won't put them on you anymore."

Later on in life, when I was older, I would think about Frank and him putting those gloves on me.

I would think, "How did Frank know? How did he know that one day I would need to know that?"

Because that second husband of mine was a fool. He was like Dr. Jekyll and Mr. Hyde. Three months after we were married, he turned into Mr. Hyde. Later I found out that he had been married twice before. So I found his second wife and called her up.

I asked her, "What is wrong with this man?"

She said she would have warned me if she knew I was coming along after her. We talked and became fast friends—great friends. And he hated it.

One afternoon, I was sitting in the kitchen getting dinner ready. I heard him come in the house. I looked up as he came walking in the kitchen carrying a billy-club. What he didn't know was, that I had gotten this little, solid wood baseball bat that I kept hidden. So I kept my eye on him. But he didn't try anything that day.

The next day, I was sitting at the kitchen table with my friend Jean when he came into the kitchen. He walked past me then kept walking back and forth. Now Jean knew he was crazy. I didn't have to tell her that. So she was watching him, watching me. And he thought I wasn't paying him any attention, but I was. He had his hand behind his back, so I was thinking he was holding that billy-club. But I didn't care because I had my baseball bat in my hand under the table. I was ready for him.

All of a sudden, Jean hollered out, "It's not a billy-club Louise. It's a gun!"

When she said that, I jumped up and hauled off and let him have it right upside his head with that bat. He dropped to the ground like a sack of potatoes. When he did, I pounced on him and went to work beating him with my bat. I don't know who called the police, but they came pretty quick.

They said, "All right, Mrs. King, you can let him up now—we're here."

By the time I finished with him, there was blood on the walls, on the floor . . . everywhere. The police picked him up and took him away to the hospital. He came home the next day with thirty-two stitches in his head. I know because my daughter, Serena, told me. She was changing his bandages counting the stitches. I wasn't gonna change them—I could care less.

The next day I heard him in the other room lying to his sister on the phone. He told her I had my friends, Bessie and Jean, hold him down while I beat him.

I yelled in there, "If I were as big as you, I'd tell that lie, too."

I wasn't about to let no man beat on me. And I had my brother Frank to thank for that. He had taught me better. He had taught me how to fight. My sister Martha was the lady growing up, but not me. I was rough and tumble—always climbing trees and hanging out with my brothers.

Frank married Mary Frances Miller from West Virginia, and they moved to Youngstown, Ohio. They had seven children. He worked as a mechanic and as a cook most of his life. Frank died at his home in 1991. He was seventy years old.

My brother, Edward Gartha Lewis, was named after my Uncle Gartha, my dad's brother. The family history book that you gave me at the birthday party had an error in it. I saw where your grandfather told you that he was "the best Jacks player" in the family. I turned to him at that party, and I asked him about it.

I said, "What is this I see here about you being the best Jacks player in the family? Mom was the best Jacks player in our family, not you."

He said, "Well, I was next."

I just laughed at him.

"No you weren't! I was next to Mom. And there was no way in this world you could ever beat me. I don't even know where you came in up the line there."

We all played Jacks. That was one of the things our family did in the evening, at night before going to bed. There was something else he had told you—oh yes, I remember. Ed told you about me throwing the scissors at him. Now that was true.

What happened was, I could not get paper dolls back then. So I used to make these paper dolls out of the Sears Roebuck Catalog. I would cut out the women then I would paste them onto cardboard. Then I would cut them out. I would also cut out the dresses and different clothes and put them on my paper dolls.

Do you know, just as fast as I was cutting out my dolls

Ed was sitting there tearing the heads off? I had cut out eight, maybe ten, when I looked over and saw that he had ripped all the heads off. Oh, I was so mad. Those things were tedious to cut out. And he was sitting there just grinning at me.

I was holding this pair of barber's scissors in my hand. They belonged to my dad. I wasn't supposed to be using them in the first place because he used them to cut hair. But they were nice and sharp. Well, I cut out one more paper doll and laid it down. Now I was watching him out of the corner of my eye. And he reached over, picked it up and ripped the head right off. As soon as he did, I took those scissors and stabbed them right into his knee so hard they stuck there, just shaking back and forth. You talk about scream—that boy screamed bloody murder.

Now my mother was a person who I often wondered about her reaction to things because, when she came in the room and saw those scissors in his leg, she didn't scream or shout—she just looked at me real calm like.

"Did you do that?" she asked.

"Yes, ma'am."

She didn't ask me why. She just grabbed me up and whipped me really good. That's when Ed stopped screaming and started smiling again. Then my mother reached down and pulled those scissors out of his leg, and he really let out a scream. Now, why my mother didn't pull those scissors out of his knee first before she whipped my behind, I don't know.

She poured alcohol on his wound then put a bandage on it. And that was that. I was sorry about what I did. I knew it was wrong, but it was spur of the moment. I just stabbed.

He was sneaky, your granddaddy—very sneaky. He would do little things on the sly, where nobody would notice. Once he was teasing me. I was sitting outside by the kitchen door and Ed kept sneaking up on me from around the corner, throwing things at me. Well, there was a brick there—a loose brick. I saw it, pulled it out, and waited for him to pop out from around the corner again. And just as he did, I took that brick and hit him square in the back of the head with it. Blood shot out of his nose, and he fell down. I really thought I killed him. But I stayed calm. I walked over to the rain barrel my mother kept covered right outside the kitchen door. I dipped some water out and dumped it on his face. Then I went on in the house like nothing had happened. Ed got up and came inside with blood running all down his face.

My mother said, "What's wrong with you?"

He said, "Nothing, my nose is just bleeding."

He took the hit for me that time. My brothers were always doing things like that.

Ed was the one who taught me how to shoot a gun. The first time he tried to teach me to shoot a rifle I was probably about twelve years old. I took the rifle, aimed, and pulled the trigger. The force from that rifle threw me back up against the fence and I hit the ground, stunned.

"Okay, now, let me show you how to hold it the right way," Ed said, picking me and the rifle up off the ground.

"Well, why didn't you show me the right way to start with?"

"Because then you wouldn't know what it felt like to use it the wrong way."

Ed liked to go hunting a lot when he was a boy. His best friends were his two hunting dogs. He took his dogs with him everywhere until one day some man poisoned the dogs. The man didn't want Ed hunting on his land. That broke Ed's heart. He loved those dogs.

In 1945, Ed joined the Army. He was seventeen years old at the time. He had a girlfriend, Levinia Johnson. Her nickname was Deanny. Then the two of them got married when they were both eighteen. Deanny was like a sister to me. Your daddy, Edward Gartha, Jr., was born while Ed was away in the Army. And Ed wanted to see his baby boy so bad he went AWOL. The MPs came and got him. He had to spend the next few weeks peeling potatoes as punishment.

Grandma Deanny Lewis

Ed joined the Army Reserves and worked as a nurse at the V.A. [Veterans

Administration] all week and preached on the weekends. He and Deanny added three more children to the family—William, Adena Kaye [Deekay], and Starla Jean.

Our family had some bad characters in it, but we also had a family with a lot of ministers in it over the years. Your granddaddy, when he was younger, he was one of them. That's why I carried on so bad when Deanny and Ed split up. I was so upset.

It was sad to watch. Deanny really began to suffer after that. She had been bothered by that hole in her heart all her life. She would try and get up from a chair and fall flat on the floor. It really got bad after Ed left her. I tried to get her to go see a doctor. I begged and pleaded. Finally, she did go. But by then it was too late for them to fix it. Your grandmother died way too young. She was only fifty-four years old. That's too young.

When Ed married Marge, she didn't want him to have anything to do with our family. She was White. Her kids were White. She came from a very White world. It didn't seem to matter until she married Ed. Then she was always pulling Ed further and further away from us, into that world.

It was hard for me to visit my brother after he married Marge. He lived three hours away from me for more than fifty years, but we rarely saw each other. And we rarely spoke. But now that Marge is gone, we try to see each other. We're old now, but he's still my baby brother. He's the only one of my brothers and sisters left.

*(From Aunt Bunch's Photo Album
Her brothers and sisters, her children, and her Grinage cousins)*

Chapter Nineteen: The Negro Side of the Color Line

I have been in the homes of Negroes, who live in White neighborhoods, and I have yet to find any race friction; the Negro goes about his business, the White man about his. Neither the wives nor the children have the slightest trouble.
—Booker T. Washington

Before one drop thinking, segregation, and racial integrity miscegenation laws, my great-great-great-grandparents, Cornelia, and Sylvester, lived in a society where they were free to be what they were and free to embrace all of their ancestry. With White fathers and mulatto mothers, they lived according to the customs of 1850 Pennsylvania society, which said: "If a person looks White, then he or she is White."

In light of this, Cornelia and Sylvester, and their children's children, lived as a White family, alongside other White families. In the late 1920s and '30s, however, things changed in Pennsylvania—and across the rest of the United States—with the institution the Racial Integrity Act (a miscegenation law prohibiting interracial marriage), even more stringent segregation laws, and the U. S. Census Bureau's *new* racial classification system.

Fueled by the White supremacist one-drop rule, the Census Bureau's new classification system stripped away the identities, lifestyles, and jobs of thousands of White and Mulatto families and reclassified them as Negro, which in the minds of many, if not most Americans (both White and Black) in 1930, meant *inferior.* If families were believed to have even "one drop" of black blood *(*as if that could be measured*),* they were reclassified, then removed from White society and restricted to the segregated parts of American society, with social boundaries and geographic borders that *colored people* could not cross.

This new classification system couldn't have come at a better time for White America. America had been hit hard by the Stock Market Crash of 1929, plunging it into what would become known as The Great Depression. During this time, many of the rich became poor and the poor became even poorer as jobs became scarce for White men, and even scarcer for Black men.

It was during this time—the Great Depression—that my family, under the government's new racial reclassification system, went from White to Black. But my great-grandpa Luke refused to accept his family's new classification. Instead, he packed up his family and ran away to another state, hoping to live and raise his children as he desired, in an Italian neighborhood amongst family. And this he did until 1940 when the one-drop rule and segregation caught up to him and his family, stripped them of their multiethnic and multiracial ancestry, leaving with just one—Black, which subjected them to discrimination and the segregated laws of the land.

The following is Aunt Bunch's story in her own words.

My father died in 1945. He was only sixty-six years old—not old at all. He died at home. I lived in town at the time, but I went out to help my mom take care of him after he took to his bed. Martha was working that day. I think all the boys, my brothers, were away in the service [military] at the time. I was sitting on the side of the bed, holding my dad's hand when he got really quiet. . . He stopped breathing. Then, I still think about this—I saw his spirit leave his body. It was real faint, but I could see it. It moved right past me toward the door. I could feel it, too. I could feel it pass by me. I didn't really know what I was seeing at the time. And I was still staring at the door when Momma appeared in the doorway.

"What's the matter with you?" she asked.

"He's gone, Momma. Daddy's gone."

Then Mom started to cry. She walked over and knelt down by the bed. That's when I got up and left.

My dad laid in state for three days. I slept on the floor next to his coffin. I missed him terribly. I sure loved my daddy.

We held the wake at the house, and it was a sight to see. The whole Parkview hillside, people from Eastview, from all over Clarksburg and other towns came to the funeral. There were a lot of Italians at my dad's funeral—I wondered where they all came from. I didn't know Clarksburg had that many Italians. And they all brought food and gifts with them—mostly money. You couldn't even see daddy's body cause of all the money—he was covered in it—lots of it. And the food. . .

Oh, my! We had so much food we had nowhere to put it. We had to give it away later.

At the funeral service, Estella, well, she liked to perform and fall out at funerals. She could do that "falling out in the aisle thing" better than anybody I'd ever seen, even in the movies. She would shout and perform and carry on, then she'd fall out and the boys would all run to catch her or pick her up. So there we all were at my dad's funeral, and Estella was sitting right behind me, next to Robert. I turned around and whispered to her, "Now you can act up if you want to. But we're gonna let your butt hit that floor if you fall out. We are not going to catch you."

She didn't act up too bad that day.

My mother's nickname was "Baugh." When my daughter Salina was little, she started calling my mom that. Then the other kids started saying it. My mother remarried after my dad died. She married a man named John Albert. He had a couple children of his own, who my mother raised. In 1965, my mom got real sick. They took her to the hospital. She went into a coma. She would go in and out of the coma. Every time she did, she would call the roll. She would call out all the kids' names. We were still waiting for some of the others to get there. If someone didn't answer her, she'd go back under. We had so many people in that hospital room, spilling out into the hall outside. There was this one nurse who kept working my nerves. She kept trying to make us all leave the hospital.

Finally, she came around the corner and shushed us and that was it. I had enough. "If you don't go away and leave us alone, I'm gonna throw your starched butt out that window!"

Well, that did it—she didn't bother us anymore. As a matter of fact, she started bringing more chairs for us to sit on.

I think William was the last one to get to the hospital. After he got there, Mom woke up again. She called the roll and William answered. Then she closed her eyes again. I went home at that point. I knew she was at peace. As soon as I got home, someone called from the hospital. She had died. It was June 10, 1965.

My mother and father didn't have anything to pass on to us—they didn't own anything. The only thing I had of my mother's was the Tartan her father had given her.... But that disappeared a long time ago. I think my older sister Estella might have taken it. She was always taking things—pictures, clothes, everything. If you didn't nail it down, she'd take it. I was going to get another one made, but I couldn't remember the colors.

[The colors are black and crimson red for Tipperary County Ireland, the O'Banion ancestral home.]

Our parents raised us by the skin of their teeth. I never had anything given to me. Whatever I wanted, I learned from my parents how to go out and work for it. That's the best thing they ever taught me. That's the best gift they could have ever given me.

Grandpa Edward Gartha Lewis, Sr.'s DNA Results

Courtesy of Ancestry.com

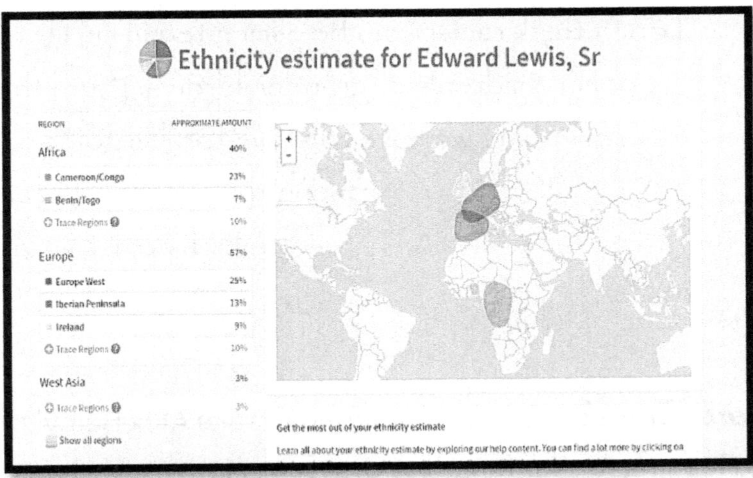

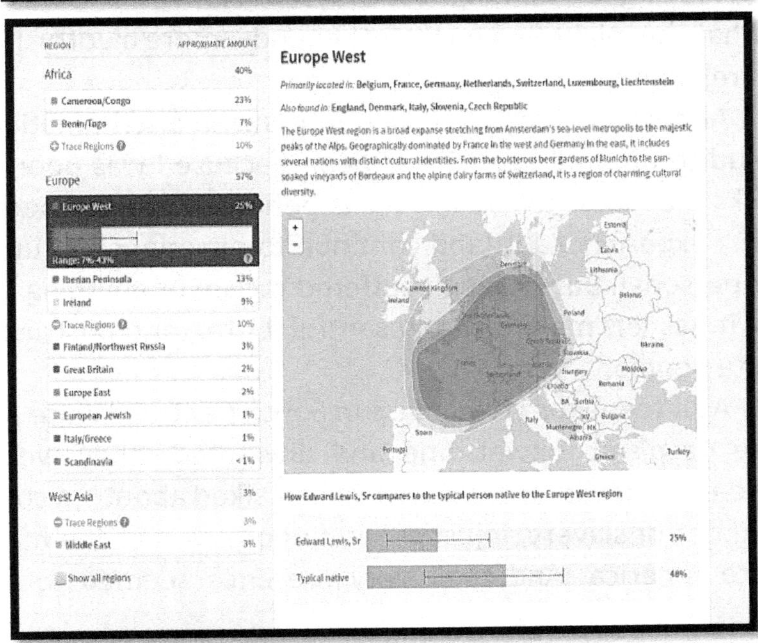

Chapter Twenty: Knocking on Doors

I don't think racism can be eliminated in my lifetime . . . or my children's or grandchildren's. But I think it's something we have to strive for. I'm going to keep working toward that day coming.
—Spike Lee, Film Director

Aunt Bunch had been too afraid to take Alex Haley's advice to go looking for her long-lost Grayson relatives. She was afraid of what she might find on the other end—more bigotry, hatred, and rejection.

Almost all of my own encounters with discrimination and prejudice up until age 15 had been because I was poor ... not Black. That's not to say I never experienced racism, because I had...I experienced it (and continue to experience it) up close and personal. But I haven't suffered racism or anything so bad that it has left me scarred, resentful, bitter, and mistrustful of White people.

As a teenager growing up in South Central, White people were despised, unwelcome and unwanted—they were the "blue-eyed devils" the Black Muslims talked about—a constant reminder of slavery, injustice, and oppression at the hands of White America. And their very presence seemed to invoke agitation or hostility.

While I could recall a few occasions in my life where racial slurs were directed at me, I hadn't lived a lifetime of struggles, injustices, and discrimination, like Aunt Bunch. That's probably why it was easier for me to pick up where she and great-cousin Grace had left off. The time had come—and I was ready, willing, and anxious to meet some of those *long-lost relatives* in Virginia ... I wasn't afraid ...Regardless their race, regardless their skin color, regardless their status, nothing intimidated me.

I couldn't wait to start knocking on doors.

My eagerness and boldness, however, was accompanied by caution. While I was ready to meet and greet some of the long-lost White relatives Aunt Bunch had referred to, I was wise enough to know that they might not be as eager to meet and greet me, especially not in Virginia. Moving to Charlottesville, Virginia, in 2001 had been an eye opener for me. And if I had ever doubted that racism and bigotry existed in the 21st Century (and I didn't), ten years of living in Virginia had made me a believer. Virginia was the birthplace of American slavery... northern Virginia was the birthplace of the famous Confederate General, Robert E. Lee...And Richmond was the former confederate capital...So I knew my venture could prove precarious. Driving from Charlottesville through the mountains and hills of Virginia, I often passed Confederate flag vendor stands along the way and homes proudly flying or hanging their Confederate flag in yards and windows, or on the side of a barn.

As a kid, growing up, I would position myself in front of the television every Friday night, at 8:00 PM sharp, to watch *The Dukes of Hazard*. It was my favorite show. I enjoyed watching the Duke boys constantly frustrate Rosco and Boss Hog as they rode around in their car, the General Lee that had a confederate flag painted on the top of it. And years later, as an adult, I was befriended by a White couple when I moved to Tennessee, who often invited me to their home for dinner where on the wall of their living room hung a Confederate flag. They were self-proclaimed *rednecks*, who considered it a symbol of southern pride. I never gave the flag another thought, and never associated it with racism...until Virginia.

In Virginia, I found the air a lot different. I quickly saw, on more than one occasion, that the Confederate flag had a different meaning. There, in the hills of Virginia, it seemed to have a different meaning...more than often it stood for separatism, bigotry, and hatred.

Despite a few confrontations and a few bad experiences with that part of Virginia culture, I was not going to let the possibility of more encounters stop me from knocking on doors, so to speak. Oddly enough, I had lived right next door to Warrenton, Virginia, for seven years... completely unaware of my family history in Warrenton. I found it ironic how the search for my family history had brought me full circle, right back to the place I had called home for ten years.

Living in Oklahoma, however, made knocking on doors in Virginia a bit difficult. So, I resorted to phone calls, which saved me time and foot work and enabled me to cover more ground, faster.

After acquiring a phone directory from Warrenton, I prepared my script—what I would say to the Virginia Graysons. I needed an opening line—something simple, something to the point, something to keep them from hanging up on me. Finally, I had it.

"Hi, my name is Tracy. I am helping my great-aunt research our Grayson family history. Her great-grandmother was Cornelia Grayson. She was born in Warrenton, Virginia. I am wondering if we could be related."

Anxious, expectant, and filled with excitement, I began

calling Graysons. And I quickly realized the minister Aunt Bunch had talked to thirty-five years earlier had been right when he said, "There are lots and lots of Graysons in Warrenton." Indeed, there were and not many of them were interested in talking about the past, at least not to me. Even more of them had no knowledge of their family history. And then there were those who simply did not want to be bothered. So… after several weeks of phone calls, my excitement slowly faded. With every phone call, I cringed, expecting rejection. Then one day, I made contact with a young woman whose father and eighty-six-year-old grandmother were both Graysons and lived in Warrenton. She and her family were White. After talking for some time, we exchanged information and planned to talk again. She believed her grandmother could be very helpful. Excited, I waited for her to call me back. But weeks passed without a word back from her. I left a message, but it proved fruitless.

Contacting long-lost relatives had proved to be a disheartening waste of time. Nobody wanted to talk. And I wasn't going to beg. Frustrated, I tossed the directory aside. Several months passed before I picked it up again. It had taken some time to get my nerve back up.

Stanley

When I finally did pick it back up, I prepared myself for the same reception and rejection, which was wise because I was met with the same results—hang ups and a lack of interest. This time I was ready to quit *after only a few short hours.*

"One more call then I'm done," I told myself as I dialed the next number.

I listened hopefully to the ring of the phone, hoping.

Then, my one more phone call was answered. It was answered by Stanley Grayson, who listened patiently as I made my introduction. I talked fast, giving him an earful. Then I stopped . . . holding my breath and waiting for his response. I expected him to hang up on me, like all the others.

To my surprise, he began to talk freely about his family, often asking me questions—*for a change.* Stanley reminded me a lot of Aunt Bunch. He was funny, witty, and a straight talker. The two of us chatted on for almost an hour, like old friends.

"I'm seventy-five years old," he shared. "But when I go to restaurants, I tell people I'm ninety-five, so they'll give me a seat right away. You should see how fast they run to get me a seat. Sometimes they bring me a wheelchair."

Stanley was full of life and full of stories...*like Aunt Bunch.* Maybe it was his age that made him so easy to talk to. Either way, he made me laugh and often.

Turns out, Stanley was born in Warrenton in 1939. His parents moved the family to South Carolina when he was just a boy, so he grew up there. He moved back to Warrenton in his twenties to try and find work and got a job at a hospital where he worked for twenty-six years before retiring. The rest of Stanley's family, his parents, and sisters, stayed in South Carolina.

"I never knew my grandparents," said Stanley. "They had died by the time I got grown. My sisters still live in South Carolina, but my parents have passed on."

I told Stanley about Aunt Bunch and gave him a brief summary of my great-great-great-grandmother Cornelia Grayson's history in Warrenton. I smiled when he agreed that we might be related. But he couldn't remember his grandparent's names since they had died when he was a young boy. I offered to look into it for him.

"I'd like that a lot," he said, sounding genuinely

appreciative.

Stanley's dialect was strong—a mixture of Virginia and South Carolina. As he talked, I couldn't help but wonder what he looked like. Did he look Black? White? Mulatto? I kept trying to pick up something in his speech—a phrase, a word, or something that might give it away. But his dialect was indiscriminate...pure country. *So, I got nothing*. Stanley was a simple *southern* man.

Finally, with the suspense of not knowing getting to me, I just came out and asked... "Stanley, I hope you don't mind me asking, but... are you White or Black?"

Thankfully, he responded with a slight laugh. And I couldn't help but laugh at my own question.

"I don't use those words," said Stanley. "When people ask me what I am, I say *colored*. I've always been colored. That's what we said growing up in South Carolina. That's what I still say."

Although his answer somewhat surprised me, I wasn't shocked. I had heard it before, from my brother-in-law, who had lived in South Carolina when he was a boy. He told me there where places where people preferred the word *colored* over *Black*.

Stanley continued.

"Some of my family was so light, people thought they was White. My sisters are both real light-skinned, but me, I have dark skin. That's why we always liked the word colored. It just fit us better."

I enjoyed talking to Stanley. We wrapped up our conversation on a good note, promising to talk again soon. I told him how I wished he could meet Aunt Bunch.

"I'd love to meet her," he said, laughing. "Bring her down sometime. She sounds like a good lady. I think we'll have a good ole time. And you're always welcome here."

My conversation with Stanley left me happy, with a sense of joy and expectation. I called Aunt Bunch and told her about him.

"Oooohhh!" She exclaimed. "I'd love to meet him, too."

I promised her we'd visit.

Ben

I met Ben by accident. Our paths crossed on the internet in a family history chatroom while I was researching Grayson family history. His knowledge of Grayson history was impressive. He seemed to be the right person to help me piece together the pieces of the Cornelia Grayson history I had found scattered across archive documents and journals from Warrenton, Virginia.

I was also hoping he could add a few more pieces to the Grayson family puzzle that I was trying to put together. So I emailed him...And he responded, rather quickly. I asked him about *Frederick William Spence Grayson*, the man whose name was written in the registry next to Cornelia's. My problem was...there were numerous Frederick W. S. Graysons, spread out over 150 years. Trying to sort through which one was which had left me confused and exhausted. I had to narrow it down.

Ben was all too ready and willing to help me. It just so happened, his great-great-great--grandfather had been Peter Grayson, cousin to Frederick W. S. Grayson. He had been at it for years. That's why he knew so much. A fact he had been quick to share with me.

Ben had made considerable progress tracing the Grayson family history not only in America all the way back to the early 1700s, to Dumfries Scotland, the birthplace of Benjamin Grayson. He had invested a lot of time, effort, and money into his research. Yet he was happy to share with me. And I was all too happy to glean.

"I could talk about Grayson history all day," Ben wrote.

"Good! Because I have a lot of questions," I wrote back.

For over a year, Ben graciously responded to my emails. He was an attorney in Texas. Yet, he always took the time to answer my questions, no matter the time of day. It was nice to know someone who had invested so much time and money into his family research—*even more than me*.

As we emailed back and forth one evening, Ben surprised me with a question...a question I hadn't anticipated and wasn't prepared for.

"Tell me, "He asked. "How is your great-great-great-grandmother related to the Graysons? I don't recall a Cornelia Grayson."

His question caught me off guard, and I froze as I read it. A twinge of trepidation crept over me, and suddenly, I was at the same crossroads Aunt Bunch had been at decades before in 1978.

All I could think about was how Ben, a White-southern Texan, might react to me telling him my great-great-great-grandmother was the illegitimate freeborn Mulatto daughter of one of his prominent Grayson relatives. *Oh, and also,* I hadn't mentioned the fact that I was Black... Not because I didn't want to. But because I honestly hadn't thought about it... It had never come up.

So, I sat at my computer, nervously trying to think of a response but I couldn't. Therefore, I said nothing. I didn't answer Ben that night. And I didn't email him for a while after that.

Ben's question made me realize that he was one of those long-lost White relatives— albeit very distant. And I was one of those long-lost Black relatives. I wanted to talk more to Ben about the Graysons, but I treaded carefully. In my research, I had stumbled across some southern Graysons who had settled in Georgia and Texas—descendants of Benjamin Grayson, our Patriarch who had come to America in the 1700s. I had planned on avoiding them. My experience with racism in Virginia had made me a bit hyperaware of racism and a bit cautious when it came to Georgia and Texas. I didn't want to meet any of those Graysons. I didn't want to stir those pots. But now, as fate would have it, I was corresponding with one of them—Ben.

I recalled leaving California at age twenty-one and moving to Juneau, Alaska. I didn't know anyone there, but that didn't stop me. I wanted to go, so I went. A woman I talked to over the phone but had never met offered me a place to stay. However, when I stepped off the plane in Juneau, I quickly became aware that a Black person in Juneau was a rare sight indeed. Coming from Los Angeles, it was somewhat alarming, to say the least. I began to wonder about my house hostess, asking myself, for the first time in my life.

"What if she doesn't like Black people?"

Thankfully, my fear was short lived. My house hostess turned out to be a Tlingit Haida Alaska Native, named Mary. She and I bonded instantly and became great friends.

That was twenty-three years ago.

Now here I was, sitting at my computer, once again asking the question I had only ever asked once in my life, but this time about Ben.

"What if he doesn't like Black people?"

I tried to push away the thought, but it wouldn't go. I tried to type the words, "Hey, by the way, I'm Black," but I couldn't.

I told myself he might not even care.

But the possibility that he might, that made me uneasy. I even entertained the thought that he might not be White. Maybe I prejudicially assumed he was White...But I wasn't buying it.

I thought about Aunt Bunch and how she had felt when Alex Haley first asked her to go knocking on doors in Warrenton. I thought of how she wrestled with the thought of going. She was right, it was hard.

Until that day, I had never hedged on anything. Boldness came easy to me. At least it used to. Now suddenly, when I needed it most, it failed me. The thought of rejection *overwhelmed me*. I wanted to tell him. I made up my mind that I would. . . But later . . . much later.

Much later took two years.

I emailed Ben to tell him about the book. He was quite encouraging and wished me well. Then, without hesitating and overthinking it, I told him about my great-great-great-grandmother, Cornelia Grayson—how she had been the daughter of William Grayson, a plantation owner. His response was short and to the point.

"I am not really interested in knowing about that side of the family. I am only interested in my side."

That was the end of our conversation.

"Ohhh...kay," I thought, after reading his response. "Well, at least he was *sort of* nice about it."

That was the last time we spoke.

In the beginning, my research had been singularly focused on finding my great-great-great-grandmother Cornelia. After finding her in the registries and other library records in Warrenton, I began to sift back through the pages and pages of documents Vickie, and I had gathered. A careful reexamination of the pages revealed something new. . . Something I had missed the first time. Three other girls were listed in the registry along with Cornelia. They also carried the name Grayson. And they had similar physical and status descriptions next to their name… "light" or "bright" mulatto, female, and *free-born*."

As I read the names— "Sarah Ann, Eliza, Sallie"—I stopped suddenly as the pages of Cousin Grace's journal flashed across my mind. I quickly ran to my desk to open the journal. Turning to page one, I read through the list of Cornelia and Sylvester's children… "William, Benjamin, Susanna, Sarah Ann, Eliza Jane, Sallie. . ." That's when I noticed the pattern.

My heart started to beat fast in my chest as I sat back in my chair and looked back over the names in the registry. I had missed them the first time. The names Frederick, William, Alfred, Benjamin, Eliza, Mary, and Susanna abounded down through the generations among the Graysons, as far back as the 1700s in America.

My great-cousin, Grace, had only recorded the lineage of Grandma Cornelia's family and the birth dates and names of her children and descendants. Grace had not mentioned any of Cornelia's or Sylvester's brothers and sisters. Therefore, I wondered.

"Could these girls in the registry be Cornelia's sisters?"

It seemed more than a coincidence. They were all close in age, only a year or two apart. And they were all four "freeborn" mulattoes. The only ones on the list.

"Could their descendants be among the long-lost relatives that Aunt Bunch had heard about in Warrenton?"

The questions made me realize that my search wasn't over.

The pattern of repetitive names that had been passed down over five generations among the Grayson clan had left a trail for me to follow. Maybe that's why clans did it. I couldn't say for sure. But I thanked God for it because *it sure did help.*

I sighed deeply, recalling Virginia and being in the Mormon library, discovering Great-Grandpa Luke for the first time and wishing someone were there to share the moment with me...But now I had Aunt Bunch. So, I called her. As expected, she was even more excited than I was. She and I had grown very close in the matter of a few years.

She had become my best friend.

Chapter Twenty-One: Residue of One Drop Thinking

In slavery times, mulatto children of slave masters often suffered more abuses and beatings because of their mixed-race ancestry.
—Frederick Douglas

Here we stand in the 21st century and one-drop rule thinking is still alive and *active* (I won't say *well*) *in America and around the world*. But are racism, the one-drop rule, and segregation, bigotry, and discrimination just American problems? Has America struggled alone with these issues?

The answer, of course, is...*no*.

As a social studies professor and a student of history, I know that to say America has struggled alone with these issues and atrocities is wrong. And to say that the rest of the world does not still struggle with these issues is also wrong.

I will never forget a woman who came up to me after I had shared the story of my family at a book signing on Tinker Air Force Base in Oklahoma City. She had walked past me a few times, listening intently as I talked with other interested persons. I could tell she really wanted to talk to me, so I smiled and waved her over. But she waited. . . She waited until I was alone...then she came over. Within a few minutes we were talking like old friends, and she began to share her family's story with me. She shared how her grandfather, an American-Indian, had been half-Black and half-Indian...But he and his family had "hushed it up." She said it was back in 1930, and the family was afraid of being reclassified as Negro. She said to this day, she and her family identify only as American Indian and White. As we talked, she spoke softly, whispering at times, very hushed and very guarded, not wanting anyone to overhear the conversation.

This ladies story reminded me of my own family, who in 1930 had experienced the exact reclassification her grandfather had feared. Three generations later, the woman was still hesitant to talk about it... She was still *keeping the family secret*.

It may come as a surprise to some people...But America *did not birth racism*. It did not start here. The White Americans who crossed over into the *New World* from Britain, Ireland, France, the Netherlands, and other countries in the 1600s, 1700s, and the following centuries to settle the American colonies brought their prejudices, bigotry, and racism with them.

In the 1600's, after building their palatial plantation homes (homes similar to the plantations in their old countries), plantation owners realized that they needed resilient, durable people to work the land...people who were far more capable of coping with the harsh climate and conditions, especially in the south.

In 1732, the British established the state of Georgia with the primary purpose of settling impoverished British citizens who would work the land and supply England with rice and cotton and other agricultural products. Then in 1750, the colonial states lifted its antislavery law in order to import slaves to harvest the growing wealth of its economy.[35] Slaves proved far more profitable than any other form of labor available to the colonists, who wilted and fainted under the intense southern heat. Thus, America began to import African, Jamaican, and West Indian slaves to work their plantations.

Slave women were forced to comply with sexual advances by their masters on a very regular basis. Consequences of resistance often came in the form of physical beatings; thus, an enormous number of slaves became concubines for these men.[36] This is not to say that all of the unions between slave masters and slave women were the result of rape. Some White slave masters and Black slave women shared a genuine love and passion for each other but were forbidden to openly display their relationships.

Mulatto children were the result of many *nonconsensual* as well as *consensual* unions between slave masters and slaves. The many mulatto (mixed race) children born to enslaved Black women were subsequently classified as Negro or mulatto according to Aryan one-drop rule thinking. And these children were either relegated to slavery alongside their Negro mothers, or traded away, or sold to other slave owners in order to remove the evidence of such transgressions or indiscretions from before the eyes of their White wives and families.

Frederick Douglas, a mulatto runaway slave, who rose to become a respected statesman and journalist in the North until his death in 1895, wrote in his personal memoirs about his experience as the mulatto child of a White slave master. Douglas wrote how he, himself, had suffered abuse and countless beatings at the hands of overseers because *the Master*, his father, wanted to prove to everyone that he did not show favoritism toward Douglas.

In June 2014, an article appeared in the British newspaper, *The Telegraph* entitled, "Dido Belle: Britain's First Black

Aristocrat." It was the story of Lady Dido Elizabeth Belle, the illegitimate, mixed-race daughter of an eighteenth-century naval captain and subject of a new film.[37] The writer, Nisha L. Diu, wrote how Lady Dido had grown up in Kenwood House in north London on a palatial plantation owned by her father's uncle—the first Earl of Mansfield. The article described Lady Dido as being very privileged and being in "the top one per cent, in terms of how she lived, her allowance, her dress, her education." Diu wrote that Lady Dido was treated like one of the family at their home in Kenwood, except when they had guests, then "the Black, illegitimate daughter of a nobleman occupied a peculiar, between-stairs rank: too well-born to belong to the serving classes but too different to be wholly welcome in high society. When the Mansfield's were entertaining, Belle didn't eat with their guests."[38]

The main focus of the article was on the extraordinary fact that Lady Dido's father, a White, 24-year-old, wealthy English aristocrat and Navy officer took Dido home to England after the death of her mother and asked his extended family to raise her. And they did. The article highlighted how mixed-race children born to White fathers during slavery times were usually abandoned by their White fathers or forced into slavery along with their mothers. Very rarely did White fathers claim their children like Lady Dido's father had done.

What stood out most about Diu's article were the readers' comments at the end of the article. Although the writer stated that Lady Dido was of mixed-race, she repeatedly kept referring to her as *a Black woman* throughout the article and not as a mixed-race woman—even the article title referred to her as Black. This became the main focus of the readers, whose comments centered on why the writer kept referring to Lady Dido, a mixed-race woman, as "Black" and not as "mixed-race."

Apparently, one-drop rule thinking also exists in Britain.

The movie, *Belle,* which was based on the book, was released that same summer. Of course, I had to see it. Afterwards, I thought a lot about my great-great-great-grandmother Cornelia Grayson, who was born to a Scottish plantation owner and a mulatto mother. I thought of how precarious her situation had been... how she could have easily been treated like Frederick Douglas, who had been cast aside by his White plantation owner father. Instead, she was "free-born" at birth. And her father saw to it that she was never relegated to the cruelty of slavery.

From White to Black is not just an American story. And it is not just the story of my family. It is the story of many families, all over America, all over the world. The entire world has struggled—and continues to struggle—with racism, one-drop-rule thinking, and bigotry.

Last year, I read a news story by a reporter writing about his trip to Puerto Rico. He talked about how he had been sitting there in a bar, watching a news story about discrimination and making racial assumptions based on a person's skin color. The reporter said he turned to the man sitting next to him, who had brown skin and asked, "As a Black man, how do you feel about that?" The man looked at the reporter and replied, "I'm not Black." The reporter then wrote, "End of story!"

After my friend, Aymee, moved back to her native Peru two years ago, along with her White, American husband and their three children, I sent her excerpts of this book to review for me and to get her opinion, seeing as she had gone to graduate school in the United States and had also been a teacher.

Later, as we skyped one night, Aymee shared how, since she had been back in Peru, she could relate to the subject of my book and to my family's story. She shared how her family and friends in Peru had already labeled her son Black-Peruvian and her daughter White-Peruvian, simply because of *the shape* of their noses. She said a chubby nose labeled you *Black* whereas a straight nose labeled you *White.* I was rather surprised and said, "Noses? Really!"

Aymee's story was eye-opening for me. It showed me that one-drop rule thinking *truly* i everywhere. Around the world, people still put a lot of effort into trying to categorize and label people based on their skin color, the shape of their nose, and other and facial features. Such thinking and categorization is similar to studies in the 1890s by Social Darwinists, who collected statistics on the size of heads, the angle of foreheads, the shape of noses, and other physical measurements to determine race.[39]

In Australia, between 1910 and 1970, children of mixed-race descent were systematically abducted and separated from their native families and cultures.[40] These children became known as the Stolen Generation. And in her 1996 book, *Follow the Rabbit-Proof Fence,* author Doris Pilkington Garimara described her lifelong journey to reconnect with her stolen identity. Garimara's book broke centuries of silence in Australia and offered a voice for the *generations* of dislocated native, Aboriginal children who had been taken from their mothers for one reason—because of their mixed-race ancestry. Once removed from their homes, the children were first incarcerated in prison camps then sent to live with missionaries all over Australia. However, some of the children, those with White features, were groomed, polished, and educated in the English language and according to Australian culture, then married off to *White* spouses.

Garimara's book exposed the racial discrimination and suppression that had been suffered by an estimated over

100,000 mixed-race children at the hands of the western Australian government. Falling victim to the government's strategic relocation of mixed-race children, Garimara was stolen from her family in 1931, at the age of twelve. However, she escaped from the prison camp and began a 1,600-kilometer journey across the Australian outback in an attempt to reunite with her family. Sadly, Garimara would be twenty-five years old before she saw her mother again.

Across the United States and across countries, the opportunities to confront stereotypes and prejudice have been plenty... "You talk White" or "You don't talk Black" ...is the story of my life. I still hear it...no matter the culture, town, or community... be it Black or White.

I have shared the story of my family with people of different backgrounds, cultures, and races, in various social settings... high schools, college classrooms, conferences, and professional workshops. Then I listen as people, in turn, share with me stories about their own families. My response to each person is always the same... *"You need to write that down."*

When I think about the term, "passing for White" ... and how unfair it is to people with multiracial or biracial ancestry, I get frustrated with the perpetuation of this racist term. The phrase perpetuates Aryan one-drop rule thinking and is typical of "racial purity" ideology. "Passing for White" was considered a crime for hundreds of years and was still considered a crime up until forty years ago in states whose Aryan one-drop laws and miscegenation laws had yet to be repealed.

However, even with the repeal of such laws, *the damage had already been done*. Thousands of mulatto families had already been stripped of their mixed-race ancestry and relegated to the Negro side of the color line. Others went "undercover" so to speak, hiding and denying their Black ancestry, often earning them the contempt, criticism, and disdain of the Black community.

A person is who they are and should be free to embrace all of their heritage and ancestry. Yet, modern day mulattos are still being attacked and berated for choosing to *also* embrace their White ancestry and for *not* living their lives solely as African-American, or Black... *as Walter Plecker and other White Supremacists applaud from the grave.* Plecker's belief that "one drop of Black blood makes one Black and only Black" was and is a White supremacist lie created by White supremacists. However, their teaching still resonates across America today, especially across Black America. Its residue still covers the minds of most Americans, most of whom have never even heard of the one-drop rule.

The practice of one-drop thinking is so ingrained into American culture and our way of reasoning and thinking that we don't even notice when we perpetuate it. But we can see it in the way we mentally (*or literally*) check the "Black" or "African-American" box in our minds or on a form when we encounter a person who is mixed-race/biracial.

Such thinking continues to propel Walter Plecker's lie into the next generation, and the next, and the next. Such thinking also begs the question: if one drop of White blood *does not* make one White then how can one drop of Black blood make one Black? Thus, the ridiculousness of racism.

In 2011, American actress Halle Berry told *Essence Magazine* that she believes in the one-drop theory, therefore she feels like her mixed-race daughter is Black. Berry further added that she considers herself Black, although she is also biracial (her mother is White, and her father is Black):

If you're of multiple races, you have a different challenge, a unique

> *challenge of embracing all of who you are but still finding a way to identify yourself, and I think that's often hard for us to do. I identify as a Black woman, but I've always had to embrace my mother and the White side of who I am, too. By choosing, I've often [wondered]," Well, would that make her feel like I'm invalidating her by choosing to identify more with the Black side of myself?" (Essence Magazine, 2014)*

Berry's comments reminded me of my Aunt Deekay and were indicative of the impact the one-drop rule has had on the thinking of millions of Americans. Berry's comments also crystallized the position many modern-day mulattos have had to take regarding their identity and race.

American comedians, Key and Peele, have openly shared on their weekly TV show of the same name that they are both biracial children with White mothers and Black fathers. Yet, they also choose to identify as Black men, a common practice among multiracial and biracial families, who often seem obligated to claim Black or African-American ancestry (especially since there hasn't been a racial category for mulatto/mixed race people since 1930).

The absence of a mulatto/multiracial category on United States government forms often leaves biracial and multiracial Americans with the only option to choose an identity from one of the *five* racial categories currently recognized by the United States Office of Management and Budget (OMB): White, Black or African-American, Asian, Native American, and Latino/Hispanic.

The limitation of options has resulted in many Americans of biracial heritage identifying as Black, and only Black. Many famous Americans of biracial and multiracial parentage have also chosen to identify solely as Black or African-American, the most notable person being American President, Barack Obama, who, even though his father is Black and his mother White, identifies solely as African-American, rather than biracial.

American author June Cross shared on an internet radio program in 2015 how, for years, that she identified as Black, and only Black after being rejected and hidden away by her White mother. Cross rejected her multiracial heritage after she had been welcomed and embraced by the Black community. On the program Cross shared how even though she has since come to embrace her biracial heritage, she still identifies as Black.

Chapter Twenty-Two: Defining African-American

If you have an important point to make, don't try to be subtle or clever. Use a pile driver. Hit the point once. Then come back and hit it again. Then hit it a third time—a tremendous whack.
—Winston Churchill

In 1997, the United States Office of Management and Budget (OMB) updated the racial categories to include African-American and Latino/Hispanic but chose not to add *multiracial* as a category. Although public comments and research provided a solid basis for adding multiracial, the office received more comments and research from members of each racial group who supported *not* adding a multiracial classification. Opponents to the addition of a multiracial classification cited "inaccurate counts of their population" and "hindrances to policy development and civil rights enforcement" among their reasons for opposing a multiracial category.

However, since the number of mixed-race children in the United States has since soared in the past fifteen years, *with the number of children born to interracial couples almost doubling,* the OMB revised its standards in 2000, establishing an allowance for thirty agencies to use "multiple races" as a response category on forms requested from schools, business, and other organizations and institutions.

National, state, and local agencies now have the "all clear" from the government to use the multiple race response table below for use in civil rights monitoring and enforcement: [41]

1. American Indian or Alaska Native
2. Asian
3. Black or African American
4. Native Hawaiian or Other Pacific Islander
5. White
6. American Indian or Alaska Native and White
7. Asian and White
8. Black or African American and White
9. American Indian or Alaska Native and Black or African American
10. >1 percent: Fill in if applicable
11. >1 percent: Fill in if applicable
12. Balance of individuals reporting more than one race
13. Total

Let me highlight at this point a common mistake. While there are currently, a minimum of 195 recognized nations in the world, only four or five racial classification groups are recognized around the world (*Black, White, Asian, Indian [varying groups], Hispanic or Latino*). And whereas *Black* is a race, *African* and *American* are *not*--these are ethnicities. The word ethnicity coming from the Greek word, *ethnos,* meaning *nation or nationality* (i.e., American, African, Irish, Italian, British {English, Scottish, Welch), German, Mexican, Spanish, etc.).

Black and African-American are often used interchangeably, which causes confusion, especially among my non-Black friends, students, and coworkers, including people from other countries who often struggle to use the proper terminology.

"What should we say? ... African-American or Black? "Sometimes I say Black and people get offended," or... "I called him African-American, and he got mad at me. This one is usually what they hear from frustrated *Black* students, coworkers, and colleagues, who are of Canadian, British, Jamaican, French, and East Indian ethnicity, yet professors and teachers are repeatedly classifying or addressing them as African-American.

It would serve us all well to remember that...America is indeed a melting pot, and, as stated by my Jamaican and Canadian friends... "not all Black people in America are African-Americans."

One night, as we discussed the topic of racism and segregation in my evening social studies class, I shared this story of my family with my students, specifically how my family had been classified as White for over one hundred years then systematically reclassified as *Negro* as a result of the *one-drop rule*. After class, two of my students hung around to talk to me. I listened as they both shared stories of their own personal struggles with the one-drop rule.

One student, Karen, shared how she, as a young White mother, struggles with what to call her biracial daughter. The father of Karen's five-year-old daughter is African. Karen's daughter, with her pale White skin, straight black hair, and green eyes, reminded me of the description of my great-great-great grandmother Cornelia, whose features would have probably mirrored those of Karen's daughter.

"Black people consider my daughter Black" and "White people consider my daughter Black," Karen said.

She continued.

"Sometimes I don't know what to tell my daughter. She

looks White, but everyone else calls her Black, so I call her Black. It's confusing."

"What does her birth certificate say?" I asked, already anticipating her answer.

"It says Black."

Her answer didn't surprise me. Sadly, I had heard of such occurrences still happening in America—and often.

Another student, Terra, a 50-year-old biracial grandmother raising her biracial grandchildren, also shared how she is continuously getting into arguments with people who "keep calling" her grandchildren Black. "My grandchildren are mixed. Their mom is White, the daddy is Black." I just don't get how people can automatically look at them and call them Black, just because their skin is darker."

Terra said she had always wondered why people thought this way. "My parents were mixed, and I have light skin, but people call me Black, too. I want my grandchildren to know their entire heritage."

I watched as a coworker still checked the African-American box on the child's form even after a mother stated that her child was *biracial*. The coworker was a young Black woman in her twenties. I waited for the parent to leave then quietly pointed out to the young woman that the mother had stated that her child was biracial, expecting the young woman to change it on the form. Instead, she responded with typical one-drop rule thinking.

"Girl, please, that child is Black."

I didn't argue the point with her. But I did make a mental note.

While my story and the story of my family may not change the centuries-old problem of racial classification, my hope is that it will encourage others to evaluate their views on racial classification and its impact on families.

In 1997, when Tiger Woods said he was Cablinasian, a term he invented as a kid in an effort to acknowledge his Caucasian, Black, Indian, and Asian heritage, he was berated, chastised, mocked, and ridiculed by many in the Black community, who accused him of not wanting to be Black. But it's all about perspective. Tiger *did* say he was Black. He said he was Black *and* Asian *and* Indian *and* Caucasian. Tiger was claiming his entire multiracial ancestry and had a right to do so. Nevertheless, there were people, both White and Black, who challenged him on the issue. They considered Tiger to be *Black* and *only* Black...the same way Walter Plecker would have. Like my great-grandpa, Luke Louis, the rest of Tiger's ancestry is inconsequential . . . only the Black part matters.

The reaction in 1997 to Tiger's stance on his ethnic heritage is indicative of one-drop rule thinking in the minds of Americans. While I am not a fan of golf or Tiger Woods per se, I am a fan of freedom and a person's right to embrace the whole of their racial identity and culture without fear of retribution, scorn, and attack. As one student said after class one evening, "Somebody has to say it...Somebody has to speak up. Somebody has to say, enough is enough!"

Today, we look back in American history and shake our heads in disgust and disapproval at the cruelties and injustices invoked on people of color down through the centuries in America, specifically on the Black and Indian races in America. We look back on slavery times and are appalled at how the slave owners wiped away the African ancestry of their slaves, forcing them to speak English and giving them more socially acceptable English names.

Similarly, from 1880 to 1902, American Indian children were taken from their families and forced into boarding schools, prohibited from speaking their native languages and taught to hate who they were born to be.[42] On top of that, they were forced to adopt English names and "White men's" clothing in order to assimilate into White society and attend government schools.

As Americans, we hang our heads in shame, appalled by such treatment and condemning such past actions. *Yet, in a day and time where interracial marriages and children are more common than ever, the travesty continues...* Aryan one-drop rule thinking, and reclassification continues. While we can't relive the past, we need to learn from it so as not to repeat it.

Chapter Twenty-Three: My Roots

There are three things extremely hard: steel, a diamond, and to know oneself.
—Benjamin Franklin

In 2015, on an internet radio program called*, The Moth: True Stories Told Live*, author June Cross talked about her book*, Secret Daughter.* She began by saying... "Every family has secrets." She then shared how, in her family, *she was the secret*.

June talked about how her mother was a White farm girl from Idaho and her dad a Black musician from New Jersey. After her parents' breakup, her mother sent her away to live with a family friend, who June was told to refer to as *Aunt*.

When June was eight years old, her mother met a White actor and fell in love. Out of fear, her mother made June promise to *never* call her mother in front of people. She didn't want anyone to know June was her daughter.

June shared how she was relegated to being *just Black*. Raised by her aunt, June refused to acknowledge her multiracial identity until the day she crossed paths with Muhammed Ali. She had flown to Las Vegas to visit her mother, and while there, she accompanied her mother and step-father to a Johnny Cash concert where she was surprised to see Ali.

After being introduced, June asked Ali, "What are two

Black people like us doing at a Johnny Cash concert?"

Ali replied, "I'm from Kentucky. Where I come from, everyone listens to Johnny Cash."

That chance meeting with Muhammad Ali (an idol to Black Americans) caused June to reexamine her multiracial heritage and started her on her path to embracing the whole of her identity.

Everyone has a story. And I could relate to June's story in many ways, especially when it came to being on both sides of the color line and feeling the constant pressure to choose sides and cultures, then finally coming to the realization that I didn't have to choose between the two...that it was okay to listen to *White* music...and okay to embrace the traditions, people, and other non-*Afrocentric* things representative of my ancestral family heritage.

When I arrived in south-central Los Angeles, fresh off the bus from West Virginia, I learned, or was told, that everything I had learned about White people up to that point was completely wrong... that I was not Black enough. . . That I had to change. . . and that I needed to "get back to my roots."

Growing up in South Central as a teenager was one of the most challenging and confusing times of my life, and I spent a good part of my teenage years trying to figure out who I was, wondering why I could never quite fit in to my surroundings. The problem was... I was an articulate, brown-skinned girl, who always carried a book in her hand. Add to that my choice of pop and rock music, my choice of clothing, and my choice of friends...many of whom were White. All of these things resulted in clash with the South-Central idea of what it meant to be Black.

But...I can't point the finger solely at my L.A. friends and neighbors. I have been hearing, "You talk White" and "You don't talk Black" all of my life... in Los Angeles, in Texas, in

Virginia, in Tennessee, in Alaska, in Oklahoma... in every other city and state that I have lived in or visited.

Over the years, I could have easily become a copy of my inner-city friends, imitating and adopting the slang of the culture, their choice of music, and their style of dress. But...doing so would have meant losing my sense of self...and giving up the things I did like about myself... my love for the English language, my White family and friends, my music, and my own self-sewn, creative, albeit heavily influenced Cindy Lauper and Madonna, clothing—complete with mixed-matched shoes—all the things that made me, *me.*

Thankfully, I had a different perspective of the world than my friends who had been born and raised in South Central. For the first twelve years of my life, I had gained a perspective that kept me from believing and embracing the stereotypes and prejudices I encountered when I stepped off the bus in Los Angeles...and many other places. When it came to White people, how Black people were supposed to talk, and what music Black people were supposed to listen to, the stereotypes and prejudices "came too late for me." I knew better.

"You need to get back to your roots" my inner-city friends used to say. So, I did. It took me almost twenty-five years. But I did it...there, at my all-White college, my journey of self-discovery had begun, my journey to find answers to my lifelong questions. And at the end of that journey, I found out I had never really gotten away from my roots...that unknowingly, I had been quite faithful to them.

I had Italian, Cheyenne, Black-Seminole, African, Irish, Cherokee, Dutch, Scottish, great grandparents and grandparents, parents, aunts, and uncles. I even had a German-English step-grandmother and step-uncles and aunts. I probably would have shared this with my inner-city friends if I had known...But back then, I didn't know. The only identity I, and my family, had was that of Black –despite the fact that my family came in every shade and color of skin—from light brown to dark brown, golden tan to light skin, to pale White. The rest of our ancestry, our history, and our birth rights had been hidden from us—wiped away by racist laws legislated by the U.S. Supreme Court and acted upon by the U.S. Census Bureau in an effort to purify the White race by waging war on anyone with mixed-race ancestry.

As I read through the pages of my great-cousin Grace's journal, a sense of pride steadily grew on the inside of me. My great-great-great-grandparents, Cornelia, and Sylvester were proud and unashamed entrepreneurs, who worked hard to instill in their children a sense of pride and belief that anything was possible. This legacy had been lost for over thirty-five years, locked away in a dresser drawer, in library archives, and in the mind of my great-aunt Bunch. Thankfully, I had found it...And it was time to share it, with my family, and with the rest of the world.

I understood Alex Haley's fascination with Grace and my family history. I understood why he wanted to tell the story of my family. It truly was an amazing story to tell.

With each discovery came an appreciation and a respect for my ancestors. They had endured painful loss, heartache, persecution, and rejection as they tried hard to hold onto their freedom and to who they were...in the face of racism, segregation, and one-drop rule thinking. One drop of White blood did not make a person White, and one drop of Black blood did not make a person Black—it made that person a mulatto... a person with a rich, multiethnic, and multiracial inheritance.

In 1991, people were quickly buying up tee-shirts proclaiming, "100% Black." I was in the Air Force at the time, stationed in Colorado, when my friend Jackie came barging into my barracks room one afternoon, smiling and prancing back and forth, proudly modeling her new "100% Black" tee-shirt.

"Check this out Tracy. You should get one. They're selling fast. So, if you want one, you better go get it now."

"No. I don't need another tee-shirt."

"Oh, come on. . ." she persisted. "If you get one, then we can wear it at the same time and make a statement!"

Up to that point, Jackie was just being her typical *pushy* self. Normally, I would redirect her to something else, but her proposal earned her my full attention, with a sharp side of indignation.

"Jackie, I can't wear that shirt! And neither can you!" I quickly added.

"Yes, I can!"

"Not with that hair you can't," I said, pointing at her hair and laughing.

My accusation had surprised Jackie. But thankfully, she got the joke and laughed along with me. She was my closest friend on the base. She was also from Louisiana—a Cajun, and proud of it. Her *perm-free* straight black hair hung down past her shoulders. And her pronounced high cheek bones and accented European features reflected the French and Indian heritage she had previously and proudly boasted to me about. *Yet,* there she stood with her tee-shirt on proclaiming, "100% Black."

I think often of my great-grandmother, Louisa Welton O'Banion, who proudly displayed her embroidered Irish tartan on her wall. She knew who she was and where she was from. . . and she was proud of it.

So am I.

A people without the knowledge of their past history, origin, and culture is like a tree without roots.

—Marcus Garvey

Me and Aunt Bunch, 2014

Me, Mom, and Tina, 2016

Family Tree ~

Grayson, Grinage, Louis/Lewis

Cornelia Grayson, Born 1834 in Warrenton Virginia
Sylvester F. Grinage, Born 1824 in Pennsylvania

Cornelia Grayson married Sylvester F. Grinage in 1850 in Pennsylvania

Children:
William J. Grinage marriage *unknown*
Susanna G. Grinage married Moses Jones
Sarah Jane Grinage married William O'Banion
Children:
Louisa Jane Welton O'Banion married Luke Louis
Olive Norman (adopted niece) marriage unknown
Eliza Jane Grinage married William Henry Pride
Children:
Archie Pride (born 1875)
Sadie Pride (born 1879)
Grace Pride (born 1896) married John Wilson of NC
Daughter: Myrtle Jane (born McKeesport, PA)
Benjamin Abraham Grinage married
Beverly Grinage unknown
Cora C. Grinage married John Wesley Brown
Sylvester Grinage married Elizabeth O'Banion
Joseph Grinage married Frances Johns
Sadie Grinage married Will Gordon
Melissa Grinage married Adam Washington
Isabella Grinage married Andrew Claughton -1st marriage
2nd Marriage to Edward Barber
Lincoln Grinage married Nancy Campbell – 1st marriage
2nd Marriage to Della Dunna
Mary Grinage (adopted)
Abraham Grinage (adopted)

Cornelia Grayson Grinage died between 1875 and 1880
Sylvester F. Grinage married Levina Scott of Pittsburgh (2nd marriage); Sylvester died in New Castle, PA in 1957

<u>Blainey Louis married Josephine (maiden name unknown)</u>

Children:
Gartha Louis – married? (Died from gunshot – abt. 1930)
Luke E. Louis - married Louisa Jane Welton O'Banion
Georgey? (half-sister -unmarried (died abt. 1933)

<u>Luke Elisha Louis & Louisa Jane Welton O'Banion</u>

Children:
William Bloomy Louis married Mary VanZandt
Children: Joseph (Joe)
William Jr.
Thomas
Maurice
Mary
George
Nash
Martha Noreen Louis married Amos Perry
Children: Amos Jr.
Frederick
Luther
Martha
Timothy
Patricia
Elston
Mark
Louisa
Franklyn Oliver married Mary Francis Miller
Children: Mary Jane "Cookie"
Rodney
Frank "Bud" Jr
Frances "Chi Chi"
Marlene "Tweety"
Renee
Marsha
Robert Alexander married Virginia Harris
Children: Garry
Elaine
Sissy
Jenny
Luke E.

Louisa "Bunch" Salina Louis married Emmett Scott Wilkinson Sr
Children:
Emmett Scott, II. married Vanclee Wilkinson
Children:
Felicia Leticia Louisa married Steve Carter
Emmett Scott, III married Rose Stephens
Salina Louisa married Theodore Wilson -1st marriage (divorced)/ 2nd marriage to John Kennedy
Children:
Tina Louisa Wilson married Steve Fararr
Tami Renee Wilson married Steve Johnson
Serena Ardora married George Nunn
Children:
George, Nunn Jr. married Kandi?
Antonette Denise married Antonio Ferez (divorced)
Darius Opeo - unmarried
Noreen Lucille married Marshall Coleman -No children

Edward Gartha Louis (Lewis), Sr. married Levinia Johnson
Children:
Edward Gartha Lewis Jr.
Children:
Katina Salin Lewis married Martin Harkless
Tracy Marie Lewis
Lisa Bright (stepdaughter)
Fatima Singleton
Kimberly Ann Washington
Edward Gartha Lewis, III
Tiwanda Griffin
William "Bill" Harris Lewis
Children:
Veronica Washington
William Edward Lewis
Mark Collins Lewis
Deion Lewis
Rashawn Lewis
Michael Lewis
Germaine Lewis
Adena Kaye Lewis married Donald Scheuvront
Children:
Justin Scheuvront
Aaron Scheuvront
Erica Scheuvront
Starla Jean Lewis
Children:
Adam Lee Harris
Tyme Scott Hammond

Acknowledgments

Thank you, Father God, for the wisdom, insight, inspiration, and fortitude to complete this project. Thanks to Vickie at Warrenton Public Library who was an invaluable help to me in my research. Thanks to my sister Tina and my brother Marty, who have been so supportive of me over the years. Rodney and Denise, without you I wouldn't be me. You taught me to be myself and to think for myself. And thank you Mom, *for flipping that coin.*

This book was written for my nephews, Isaiah, Isaac, and Israel, for Aunt Bunch's grandchildren, and for the Louis family generations that are and that will be. May we never again forget our history or have it stolen from us.

About the Author

Tracy M. Lewis was born in Clarksburg, West Virginia but moved to south-central Los Angeles, California at the age of twelve. She has lived in eight different states, including Texas, Colorado, Tennessee, Alaska, and Virginia. Her work and desire to experience other cultures has also taken her to other countries. Lewis is a veteran of the USAF and has worked and served as an elementary and middle school principal, social worker, administrator, and youth pastor. She currently resides and works as a professor in Tulsa, Oklahoma.

Other books by Dr. Lewis available on Amazon:

- *Into the Wilderness: A Journey of Faith*
- *Into the Wilderness: Battle Ready*
- *The Truth about Angels: Hollywood versus the Bible*
- *Before the King: The Story of Two Mothers*

Contact Information:
tlewisauthor@gmail.com
(20+) Tracy M. Lewis | Facebook

Photograph Credits

Page 3 – Photo of Aunt Bunch and Tracy in 2014
Page 21 – Photo of my Aunt Deekay's three children: Justin, Aaron, and Erica
Page 22 – Photo of Grace Grinage Pride and her daughter, Myrtle Jane Pride
Page 35 – Photo of Rodney Hilson playing drums
Page 54 – Photo of Rodney in front of one of my bedroom walls in the 1980s
Page 67 – Photo of my maternal great-grandmother, Stella Marie Hardy
Page 68 – Photo of Tracy and Tina in West Virginia, ages 5 & 6 (?)
Page 94 – Photograph of Clarksburg, West Virginia, by Tim Kiser. Permission details: I publish this photograph according to the terms of the Creative Commons Attribution Required / Share Alike License 2.5. Retrieved from http://en.wikipedia.org/wiki/Clarksburg,_West_Virginia
Page 96 – Photo of my grandfather, Edward Gartha Lewis, Sr. when he was younger (date unknown)
Page 101 – Photo of Aunt Bunch and her brother (my grandpa) Edward Gartha Lewis in 2006
Page 109 – Photo of Aunt Bunch on her porch in Martinsburg, West Virginia
Page 120 – Photograph of map of Warrenton, Virginia
Page 136 – Photograph of Elizabeth Dohrmann Thaw. Photographer unknown.
Page 137 - Photograph of Lillian Russell, 1897" by Unknown - Google Books - (1897-11). "Copyright or Blackmail?" Fame VI: 385. Licensed under Public Domain via Wikimedia Commons - http://commons.wikimedia.org/wiki/File:Lillian_Russell,_1897

.png#/media/File:Lillian_Russell,_1897.png
Page 154 - Photograph of Westmoreland Coke Ovens Burning by Mammoth Mines and Coke Works. Retrieved from Virtual Museum of Coal Mining in Western Pennsylvania at http://tinyurl.com/pjbhozv
Page 155 - Photograph of Man Firing a Coke Oven by Hostetter Mine & Coke Works, Lippincott Mine & Coke Works, Jamison No. 21 Mine. Hostetter Unity Township, Westmoreland PA, USA. Retrieved from Virtual Museum of Coal Mining in Western Pennsylvania, http://tinyurl.com/ozcvytu
Page 165 – Photograph of my paternal great-grandparents, Louise Welton O'Banion and Luke Elisha Louis
Page 166 – Photo of Louise "Bunch" King at home in Martinsburg, WV
Page 167 - Photograph of Senator Ben Nighthorse Campbell. This United States Congress image is in the public domain. This may be because it is an official Congressional portrait, because it was taken by an employee of the Congress as part of that person's official duties, or because it has been released into the public domain and posted on the official websites of a member of Congress. As a work of the U.S. federal government, the image is in the public domain. Retrieved from http://www.doi.gov/news/04_News_Releases/campbell.htm
Page 180 – Photograph of a Chicago rally of the Ku Klux Klan in the early 1920s. Retrieved from Smithsonian Magazine image in the public domain.
Page 181 – Photograph of the Blackhand in West Virginia. There are no known copyright restrictions on the photographs in the George Grantham Bain Collection. **Access:** Permitted; subject to P&P policy on serving originals. **Reproduction (photocopying, hand-held camera copying, photoduplication**

and other forms of copying allowed by "fair use"): No known copyright restrictions. Prepared by Prints and Photographs Division staff. Prepared: December 20, 2001. Last revised: Nov. 2015. Retrieved from http://www.loc.gov/pictures/item/ggb2004003246/
Page 188 – Photograph of 1940s Pike Street, uptown Clarksburg WV. Photographer unknown - Retrieved from https://www.google.com/search?q=pictures+1940s+clarksburg+west+virginia&espv=2&biw=1920&bih=935&tbm=isch&tbo=u&source=univ&sa=X&ei=Xt1gVcTYAcacNpnvg8AO&ved=0CCgQ7Ak#imgrc=_
Page 190 - Photograph of Kelly Miller High School. This image (or other media file) is in the public domain because its copyright has expired. This media file is in the public domain in the United States. This applies to U.S. works where the copyright has expired, often because its first publication occurred prior to January 1, 1923. See http://copyright.cornell.edu/resources/publicdomain.cfm for further explanation. Retrieved from http://en.wikipedia.org/wiki/Kelly_Miller_High_School
Page 190 - Photograph of Scientist - Kelly Miller, by the Kelly Miller Association. This work has been released into the public domain by the copyright holder. This applies worldwide. Retrieved from http://en.wikipedia.org/wiki/Kelly_Miller_High_School#/media/File:Kelly_Miller.jpg
Page 200 - Photograph of 1940s Street Car in Clarksburg, West Virginia. Retrieved from https://www.google.com/search?q=pictures+1940s+clarksburg+west+virginia&espv=2&biw=1920&bih=935&tbm=isch&tbo=u&source=univ&sa=X&ei=Xt1gVcTYAcacNpnvg8AO&ved=0CCgQ7Ak#imgrc=_
Page 202 – Photos of Grandpa Ed and other members of the

Most of the photographs in this book are from my personal collection.

References

[1] One-drop rule. (2015, March 1). In *Wikipedia, The Free Encyclopedia.*

[2] Talbot, T. Walter Ashby Plecker (1861–1947). (2014, May 30). In Encyclopedia Virginia. Retrieved from http://www.EncyclopediaVirginia.org/Plecker_Walter_Ashby_1861-1947.

[3] United States Holocaust Memorial Museum. The Holocaust: A Learning Site for Students. Nazi Racism. Retrieved on March 10, 2018 from https://www.ushmm.org/outreach/en/article.php?ModuleId=1000767 9

[4]Snipp, C. Matthew: Stanford University & Lieber, Carolyn A.: University of Minnesota. *The End of the One-Drop-Rule.* http://paa2012.princeton.edu/papers/121933

[5] Shmoop Editorial Team. (2008, November 11). *Law in Jim Crow.* Retrieved February 17, 2015 from http://www.shmoop.com/jim-crow/law.html

[6] Shmoop Editorial Team. (2008, November 11). *Law in Jim Crow.*

[7] Pauli Murray, ed. States' Laws on Race and Color (Athens, 1997), 428, 173, 443, 37, 237, 330, 463, 22, 39, 358, 77, 150, 164, 207, 254, 263, 459.

[8] Desmond-Harris, J. The Horrible Awkwardness That Ensues When You Mistake Someone's Race on National TV. *(March 18, 2015)* In *VOX Express.* Retrieved from http://www.vox.com/2015/3/18/8244605/jay-smooth-race-Black

[9] Elijah Muhammad. (2015). In *Encyclopædia Britannica.* Retrieved from http://www.britannica.com/biography/Elijah-Muhammad

[10] Bolaffi, Guido. (2003). Dictionary of Race, Ethnicity and Culture. SAGE, 200, pages 270-271, Retrieved from Google Books on July 20, 2015. https://books.google.com/books?id=ZgaNjbesx-gC&pg=PA271&dq=marcus+garvey+view+on+territorial+segregation&hl=en&sa=X&ved=0CEgQ6AEwB2oVChMImpeyk63qxgIVEJSICh1AmwFs#v=onepage&q=marcus%20garvey%20view%20on%20territorial%20segregation&f=false

[11] Ernst, Douglas. Louis Farrakhan calls for American flag to come down: 'Who

are we fighting today?'
The Washington Times - Thursday, June 25, 2015 Retrieved from http://www.washingtontimes.com/news/2015/jun/25/louis-farrakhan-calls-american-flag-come-down-who-/

[12] Ernst, Douglas. Louis Farrakhan calls for American flag to come down: 'Who are we fighting today?'

[13] Editors et al., *Separate Is Not Equal: Brown v. Board of Education*. (Smithsonian National Museum of American History, 2004), Retrieved on July 12, 2014 from http://americanhistory.si.edu/brown/history/1-segregated/jim-crow.html

[14] Lawson, Terry. Belle Aire Plantation. Prince William County, VA. http://www.rootsweb.ancestry.com/~vapwilli/history/grayson.shtml

[15] Fazzini, P. *Capt. Benjamin Grayson*. (Family Search, August 31, 2015) Retrieved from https://familysearch.org/photos/artifacts/18779600

[16] Barton, David. *George Washington, Thomas Jefferson & Slavery in Virginia*. (Wallbuilders: Issues and Articles, January 2000) Retrieved from http://www.wallbuilders.com/libissuesarticles.asp?id=99

[17] *Colonial Virginia Statistics: By the number.* Retrieved on April 2014 from http://www.shmoop.com/colonial-virginia/statistics.html

[18] Turner, Edward R. *The Abolition of Slavery in Pennsylvania.* (The Pennsylvania Magazine of History and Biography, Vol. 36, No. 2, 1912), 129-142. URL: http://www.jstor.org/stable/20085586 .Accessed: 17/09/2012 17:09

[19] Turner, *The Abolition of Slavery in Pennsylvania.*

[20] City of Monongahela, *History of the City of Monongahela 1769*. Retrieved on September 17, 2012 from http://www.cityofmonongahela-pa.gov/History.htm

[21] Turner, *The Abolition of Slavery in Pennsylvania.*

[22] Woodson, Carter G., *Free Negro Heads of Families in the United States in 1830.* (Publisher: Association for the Study for Negro Life and History, Inc., Washington, DC), 26-30.

[23] Woodson, Carter G., *Free Negro Heads of Families in the United States in 1830.*

[24] Lombardo, P. *Eugenic Laws Against Race Mixing*. University of Virginia. Retrieved from http://www.eugenicsarchive.org/html/eugenics/essay7text.html

[25] Moore, Jacqueline M. (2003). Booker T. Washington, W.E.B. Du Bois, and the Struggle for Racial Uplift. Social Darwinism. Rowman & Littlefield, Jan 1, 2003 Retrieved on July 20, 2015 from https://books.google.com/books?id=F713hEvIOAgC&pg=PA1&dq=web+dubois+view+on+segregation&hl=en&sa=X&ved=0CDkQ6AEwBWoVChMIpLq0xrbqxglVg1mSCh0IAwlm#v=onepage&q=web%20dubois%20view%20on%20segregation&f=false

[26] One-drop rule. (2015, March 1). In *Wikipedia, The Free Encyclopedia*. Retrieved 00:19, March 8, 2015, from http://en.wikipedia.org/w/index.php?title=One-drop_rule&oldid=649419984

[27] Fiske, W. *The Black-and-White World of Walter Ashby Plecker.*

[28] Cortes, C. E. (2013) Multicultural America: A Multimedia Encyclopedia, Volume 1. Sage Publications pg. 1378. Retrieved from https://books.google.com/books?id=VQ1zAwAAQBAJ&pg=PA1378&lpg=PA1378&dq=what+happened+to+interracial+couples+already+married+under+the+racial+integrity+act&source=bl&ots=tVWSICp28q&sig=mvRvRGLKNrz2yyPWMjp0FKESwZ0&hl=en&sa=X&ei=QL5OVZtqhJg2jv2AiAc&ved=0CFAQ6AEwBw#v=onepage&q=what%20happened%20to%20interracial%20couples%20already%20married%20under%20the%20racial%20integrity%20act&f=false

[29] One-drop rule. (2015, November 8). In *Wikipedia, The Free Encyclopedia.*

[30] Talbot, T. Walter Ashby Plecker (1861–1947).

[31] Spiro, Jonathan. (2009). Defending the Master Race: Conservation, Eugenics, and the Legacy of Madison. University of Vermont Press, p. 255. Retrieved on July 20, 2015 from https://books.google.com/books?id=H7lRrClcsncC&printsec=frontcover#v=onepage&q=sterilization%20&f=false

[32] One-drop rule. (2015, March 1). In *Wikipedia, The Free Encyclopedia.*

[33] Smith, J. Douglas. The Campaign for Racial Purity and the Erosion of Paternalism in Virginia, 1922

1930: 'Nominally White, Biologically Mixed, and Legally Negro. *Journal of Southern History* 68, no. 1 (February, 2002): 65–106, accessed 26 August 2011.

[34] Murray, Pauli, ed. *States' Laws on Race and Color* (Athens, 1997), 428, 173, 443, 37, 237, 330, 463, 22, 39,

358, 77, 150, 164, 207, 254, 263, 459.

35 Sumpter, Althea. *Geechee and Gullah Culture*. (March 31, 2006). Georgia Institute of Technology. Retrieved on July 21, 2015 from http://www.georgiaencyclopedia.org/articles/arts-culture/geechee-and-gullah-culture

[36] Sterling, Dorothy. (1997). We Are Your Sisters: Black Women in the Nineteenth Century. W. W. Norton & Company; Reissue edition. Retrieved on July 25, 2015 from http://www.bowdoin.edu/~prael/projects/gsonnen/page4.html

[37] Diu, Nisha L. Dido Belle: Britain's First Black Aristocrat. (June 6, 2014). In *The Telegraph*. Retrieved from http://www.telegraph.co.uk/culture/film/10863078/Dido-Belle-Britains-first-Black-aristocrat.html

[38] Diu, Nisha L. Dido Belle*: Britain's First Black Aristocrat.*

[39] Moore, J. (2003). Booker T. Washington, W.E.B. Du Bois, and the Struggle for Racial Uplift. Scholarly Resources Inc., p. 3.

[40] Gudmundsdottir, Jona G. The Stolen Generations: Racial Discrimination and the Reclamation of Identity in Doris Pilkington Garimara's *Follow the Rabbit Proof Fence.* B.A. Essay, May 2012. Retrieved on May 8, 2014 from http://skemman.is/stream/get/1946/11506/28586/1/J%C3%B3na_Gu%C3%B0r%C3%BAn_Gu%C3%B0mundsd%C3%B3ttir_BA_Essay_2012.pdf

[41] Office of Management and Budget. OMB BULLETIN NO. 00-02 - Guidance on Aggregation and Allocation of Data on Race for Use in Civil Rights

Monitoring and Enforcement. (March 9, 2000). Retrieved on August 1, 2015 from https://www.whitehouse.gov/omb/bulletins_b00-02/

[42] Public Broadcasting Station (PBS). (2006). Indian Country Diaries: Indian Boarding Schools. Retrieved on July 29, 2015 from http://www.pbs.org/indiancountry/history/boarding2.html

Made in the USA
Middletown, DE
06 August 2021

45117997R00136